NICOLA MORGAN

WALKER
BOOKS

First published 2023 by Walker Books Ltd
87 Vauxhall Walk, London SE11 5HJ

2 4 6 8 10 9 7 5 3 1

This book has been typeset in Eureka Sans Pro

Printed in Great Britain by CPI Group (UK) Ltd
Croydon, CR0 4YY

British Library Cataloguing in Publication Data: a catalogue
record for this book is available from the British Library

ISBN 978-1-5295-1256-4

www.walker.co.uk

MIX
Paper | Supporting
responsible forestry
FSC® C171272

CONTENTS

INTRODUCTION

THIS BOOK AND YOU

There are eight billion people in the world, each with different worries, different lives, different support and different reactions to the worries in their head. Just for the moment the one who matters most among all those billions is you. You are the one I'm writing this book for. And you have more than ten times eight billion brain cells, connecting together in ways that make you unique and forming the thoughts, worries, fears and dreams in your mind.

Maybe you're someone who worries a lot about small things. Or you worry about big things that will probably never happen. Or maybe you have certain things that worry you more than they worry other people. Whatever your personality, however your mind works and whatever the size and number of your worries, I aim to help you live your life bravely, confidently, wisely and well. I will show you that, however powerful your worries sometimes feel, you are stronger than them, you are worth more than them and you can deal with them.

No Worries will reduce the strength of your worries and hand the power back to you.

Maybe you are going through something really scary – something that is making you anxious, fearful, distressed. You might think it's too big to manage and that you'll always feel like this, that you have no power. I will show you that even when you can't change what's going on around you, you can change how you cope with it. And that you can even grow from it and be stronger for your future.

No Worries will help you to respect yourself, to acknowledge that you're going through something tough but that you will get through it and there will be light ahead.

Maybe you're a person who doesn't worry very much but you live with or care about someone whose anxieties are causing them distress. You probably want to know how to understand and help them. You might well be worried about them even if you're not much of a worrier yourself.

No Worries will help you understand all you need to know about anxiety, how it affects people and how you can help deal with it in anyone you care about – including, first, yourself.

No Worries is not a magic wand, able to change the things that happen to you. It is better than that: it will change *you*. You will be able to face the things you worry about, and say to yourself that there are no worries strong enough to keep you down or bad enough to stop you living a good, valuable, successful and happy life.

THIS BOOK AND ME

I decided to write *No Worries* for three reasons. First, I discovered that in 2021 the word "anxiety" was recorded as the most common word young people use when talking about health and well-being (in a survey by Oxford University Press). That worried me! But I have the solutions and I wanted to share them with you.

Second, I believe that many people are too anxious about anxiety and that a different way of seeing it would help them manage their lives more positively, more usefully and more happily.

Third, I am a big worrier myself but I've learnt a LOT over the years about how to keep the worries under control. I've come to understand the science and I see anxiety as an important part of human experience, but one that we do need to learn to manage if we are to live our best possible lives. It's not always easy but, like any skill, we get better at it when we take the right steps.

As it happens, right now, I have a really big worrying thing going on in my life. My anxiety is sky-high. But I have been reminding myself: it's OK, normal, natural, *right* to experience anxiety when something distressing is happening. It's my brain and body reacting entirely correctly and all I have to do is manage my breathing, my heart rate and whatever else my body is doing, and I will be fine. You can read a bit more about my personal experiences on page 32 and also on page 187.

The problem with anxiety is not anxiety itself, but how the anxious person reacts to anxiety. This book will help change and improve your reactions. Writing it, especially while going through extreme worry and stress, improved my reactions further. I thought I knew it all and then I discovered there was more. We learn all the time!

HOW THIS BOOK WILL HELP

No Worries will show you how to understand anxiety – what it is and what it does. I'll show you that it's not an enemy. It's more like a guard dog that sometimes reacts to the wrong things or overreacts. Sometimes, it forgets who it's meant to be guarding and growls at its owner – you – and scares or distresses you instead of protecting you. It's only doing that because either it has experienced bad things in the past, which is not its fault, or because it has not yet been well-trained. I'll show you how to work with and train your guard dog so that it is perfectly tuned to keep you safe and strong and allow you to enjoy life confidently and fully.

Anxiety is not itself an illness, although it has mental and physical symptoms that don't feel pleasant. And it can sometimes make you feel ill. After a while, it can develop into an illness – an anxiety disorder – when it really gets in the way of you living your best life. You will learn more about that in this book.

It can be difficult to tell when healthy and reasonable levels of anxiety have tipped into illness. Some people believe they are ill when they are just feeling uncomfortable – because anxiety always feels uncomfortable. Judging whether your anxiety is within acceptable or appropriate levels or not, and whether you need professional help or can deal with it by yourself, is not easy. This book will help you make that judgement.

HOW THIS BOOK WORKS

There are three main parts to your journey through this book:

Part One: Anxiety and YOU

You will look at whether anxiety is a relatively big or small part of your life. What sorts of things are worrying for you? Is your anxiety constant or triggered by certain events? How can you tell when anxiety is becoming a problem, becoming too much? Everyone's different, so this section will help you see where you are compared to some of the people around you. (Note: there is no competition! However seriously or slightly you are affected by worries, you are important and I can help.)

Part Two: All About Anxiety

What is anxiety? What's going on in a person's brain and body when a worry arrives? What is the biology of anxiety? How does it affect people? When you really understand anxiety, there are two main benefits: first, you stop seeing anxiety as a scary enemy; and, second, the strategies I offer you will make more sense and be easier to stick to.

Part Three: Strategies and Solutions

You will discover techniques for dealing with anxiety, facing challenges bravely and being able to relax when you want or need to. This is by far the biggest and most important section but you do need the first two if you want to benefit fully and be able to choose the right strategies for yourself. This section is also organised specially so that you can go quickly to the right sort of strategy for what you personally are experiencing and if you don't read the first two parts, you won't understand that.

At the end, you'll find some real-life stories from people who generously shared their own experiences with anxiety, either when they were younger or into their adult lives. I hope these will help you see how normal and human it is to suffer from unpleasant anxiety sometimes and how we can all become expert in dealing with our own responses.

Overall, you will learn to detect anxiety before it gets too much, so you can confidently put it back in its box – your guard dog in its kennel! – and do your best in life. You will learn how you can be bigger and stronger than your anxious thoughts and how calmness can be your superpower.

Life is like a mountain range. You can choose to worry what might be (but probably isn't) over each peak and forget to be amazed by the fantastic view along the way. Or you can choose to be excited, embrace life and breathe the beautiful air every step of the journey. You can choose to avoid everything you're worried about or you can grasp each opportunity and live the ups and downs with courage and excitement. You might not think you can choose, but you can.

When anxiety becomes your trained guard dog, not your scary monster, you will be able to do just that. This book will show you how to do that training.

PART ONE
ANXIETY AND YOU

Every human gets anxious sometimes. Literally everyone. Not everyone recognises their anxiety and some people might even pretend it never affects them. Sometimes, a person keeps their anxiety hidden while a bad thing is happening and then it hits them later, when the upset is over. And not everyone feels anxious about the same things or at the same time or in the same way. But every human experiences anxiety at some point and there will be lots of people who experience it just as much and in the same way as you. In Part Two you'll understand why what I've just said has to be true. For now, let's just focus on you.

Specifically, let's focus on you now, rather than you in general. Your anxiety and how it affects you now is not how it will be all your life. Or maybe even tomorrow. It will even change as you read this book – partly because this book is written deliberately to change your relationship with anxiety! Anxiety is triggered by things happening around you and things inside your head, and those things change daily, hourly, constantly. The starting point is recognising how you are now.

If you're not feeling particularly anxious at the moment, you can also use the questions I'm going to ask you to recognise the signs next time you do experience worry.

We can't control something until we know how to identify it correctly, so let's do that first. The next few pages ask you lots of questions which you need to think about carefully. You can write the answers on paper or on a screen or you can just keep them in your head. Don't write in this book, though: you need your answers to be private and someone else might want to read the book!

QUIZZES TO ASSESS YOUR RELATIONSHIP WITH ANXIETY

QUIZ 1: ARE YOU A BIG WORRIER?

This quiz will help you see where you fit on the scale of "generally highly anxious person" to "generally very calm person". It will also help you to feel less alone, because I promise you that not one of the statements in the quiz is at all unusual.

Anyone might feel very worried sometimes because whoever you are, sometimes really big worries come along, and we are all affected by what's happening in our lives. If we weren't, we wouldn't be human.

Some people are big worriers about smaller things, things that others might not worry about. And some people are quite calm some of the time but have phases when worries feel overwhelming. Some people keep their worries more hidden than others but can still be very worried inside. Let's start to see where you fit in that picture.

How you answer these questions today might not be exactly the same as how you would tomorrow or next week or next month, because feelings and thoughts change all the time. But this quiz is trying to detect a general picture of how you currently feel.

Choose the response that fits you best, even if it doesn't exactly describe you.

1. **How do you believe your anxiety compares to how the rest of your age group experiences it?**
   a. I seem to be more anxious in general than my friends and peers.
   b. I'm probably more anxious than some and less anxious than others.
   c. I would say that most or many people my age seem more anxious than me.

2. **How often do you feel anxiety is a problem for you?**
   a. I feel anxious about something most days or every day.
   b. I can go through many days without feeling anxious but then many days when I do.
   c. It's only occasionally a problem, for example when I have a test coming up.

3. **Is anxiety spoiling your enjoyment of life?**
   a. My feelings of anxiety affect me badly most or every day. I sometimes miss out on opportunities because of this.
   b. I'd rather be less anxious but it doesn't stop me doing my best.
   c. It's really not a problem. Just a bit uncomfortable but that's natural. But it would be nice never to feel anxious!

4. **Do you experience panic attacks?**
   a. I have more than once felt so panicky that I needed to escape the situation. I felt I was going to die.
   b. I sometimes feel panicky in a very stressful situation but I soon manage to take control. Probably no one else notices. It's not nice but not the end of the world.
   c. Not panic exactly. If I have a very scary thing like a performance coming up I can feel highly stressed, but it doesn't stop me performing well.

5. **What kinds of things make you anxious?**
   a. All sorts of things: whether I've said the wrong thing, failing a test, someone not liking me, worrying that someone I love might be ill, or I might be ill. Any time I hear a sad story in the news I worry about it happening to me. A lot of my worries are not about things that are really happening – it's mostly "what if?"

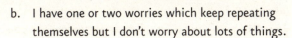

b. I have one or two worries which keep repeating themselves but I don't worry about lots of things.

c. Mostly things that are actually happening in my life. So, if someone's ill or I have exams or stressful things ahead. I don't tend to spend much time worrying about things in the past or things that probably won't happen.

6. How reasonable do you think your worries are?

a. I often feel that I am much more anxious than I should be. I can get incredibly worried about something small and afterwards it seems ridiculous that I was so worried. Sometimes when I tell people my worries they laugh at me.

b. I feel that my worries are mostly reasonable. If something really big is happening, I might get very worried but when it's a small thing my anxiety is much less. And once the stressful thing is over, I relax.

c. I believe my anxiety is at a reasonable level for the things that are happening around me. Obviously, I get worried if something really stressful is happening but I soon get it under control. I don't fret much about things I can't control.

7. How do you see your anxiety levels now compared to when you were aged eight or nine?

a. I was a big worrier at that age but I'm definitely more so now.

b. When I was younger, my life seemed like one big game – there's more to worry about now, naturally.

c. That's a long time ago – I don't really remember! But I think I've always been quite laid-back, to be honest. And as I get older, I'm getting more control over my life.

8. **Do you have some major difficult things happening in your life at the moment? This might be family illness, your own illness, parental break-up, money worries for your family, mental illness (you or someone close), struggles at school, friendship problems or something similarly stressful.**
   a. Yes, I am going through a really worrying life event.
   b. No, I don't have any of those big problems but I do still have the normal pressures for my age, such as exams or sometimes arguments with the adults in my household.
   c. No, my life is pretty OK right now.

9. **What role models or support do you have for managing anxiety well?**
   a. Some of my friends and family members suffer from anxiety and I don't think the adults around me are in a good place to help me.
   b. I do see some people around me being very anxious, but I also have at least one person close to me who I think has a healthy attitude and I can turn to them if I need help.
   c. I am very lucky to have people I can turn to. Either my school, my friends or my family can help.

10. **How much would you benefit from dealing with anxiety better?**
    a. I am desperate to feel less anxious – it really is a big problem for me.
    b. I think I would benefit from being able to manage anxiety better.
    c. I think I'm fine right now but I'd like to learn some skills so I could help other people who suffer from anxiey.

WHAT YOUR ANSWERS MEAN

You've probably already worked out that the "a" answers indicate higher levels of anxiety and "c" answers suggest a lower level of anxiety.

The good news is that, whatever your answers are, they are all completely natural and they do not necessarily mean that you are ill or have an anxiety disorder. There are lots of people who would have answered exactly as you did.

The more "a" answers you gave, the more it seems as though your quality of life is being reduced by your anxiety levels. This book will help you! You might benefit from further professional help or you might manage perfectly well using this book, along with other good advice and the support of people around you. Don't forget to check the Resources on pages 197–203 for more help, too.

The "b" answers are "middle of the road" responses that don't indicate that you're being badly affected by anxiety. You'd probably like to feel even better, though? Although anxiety is natural, it's not pleasant and it can interfere with well-being.

If you answered "c" to lots of questions, you are very lucky! There are various possible reasons why you might be less anxious than some other people:

✴ Perhaps you've not had many big distressing events in your life.

✴ Perhaps you've had lots of support and good role models.

✴ You might have a naturally calm personality.

✴ Your life is going smoothly at the moment and over recent months.

Value those positives about you and your life. Keep looking after yourself and do read the advice in this book so you can help yourself when you do experience anxiety, or if you want to understand and help others.

SOME THINGS TO THINK ABOUT

⋆ All the questions asked for your own personal reaction and that will be affected by your current mood or mental state. So, if you're feeling anxious or negative right now, you probably answered in a more negative way than if your mood was more upbeat. In this book, you'll learn that anxiety is about perception and reaction, more than external reality.

⋆ Your answers do not give a medical diagnosis. If you are concerned, you should talk to a professional. Ask a trusted adult where to start.

HOW TO USE THESE INSIGHTS

What you've learnt about yourself here is a great starting point. It helps you have a sense of where your own anxiety levels are, what pressures there are in your life and also to have some ideas of how to describe and talk about worries. As you work through this book, and especially in Part Three, you'll find lots of suggestions about how to feel better and to manage your worries healthily. You might also want to go to page 187 and read the personal stories from people who have experiences of anxiety in their lives. We often learn about ourselves by understanding other people more.

It's easy to say "no worries" but it takes some practice to make it work! If you are naturally somewhat anxious, don't expect to achieve the "c" answers, or at least not straightaway, but aim to move towards more "b" answers. This book will help you do that. There is nothing at all wrong with feeling anxious sometimes. All we want to do is make anxiety manageable when it's there and allow you to relax and have fun when it's not. We want to train your guard dog to growl at the right things.

Now let's look at how you personally react to whatever worries you have: first how your body reacts, then how your mind reacts.

QUIZ 2: HOW DOES YOUR BODY REACT TO ANXIETY?

Anxiety begins in your brain, but your brain affects every part of your body. So, the effects are felt in various parts of your body, not just your brain. We're all a bit different in how we react but you will certainly feel some of the same things as other people. But don't be surprised or worried if you experience anxiety differently from someone else you talk to.

It's important to notice what anxiety does in your body. On the list below you might find some things you didn't realise can be caused by anxiety and it's reassuring to know that that's all they are: not a serious illness but the body's natural stress responses (which you'll learn more about in Part Two). Once you spot the signs, you can step in and use some of the strategies in Part Three, before the problem grows. And your particular signs of anxiety will point you towards the right strategies for you.

Think carefully when you read the list because it's possible that you've been experiencing these symptoms without realising that you're anxious. For example, people often worry about their repeated headaches or stomach-aches and are surprised and reassured to realise that they're often just caused by stress and not something more serious. (You should always get physical symptoms checked by a doctor if they last more than a couple of weeks, though.)

Which of the following physical things happen to you when you are nervous or anxious about something? For example, when you are about to perform in public, do an exam, take part in a competition or be in a situation where you'll meet lots of people.

    a.   I feel nauseous and it's difficult to eat.

    b.   When I do eat, I am likely to choose very sweet, salty or fatty things like chocolate and crisps.

    c.   I get stomach-aches or abdominal pains.

d.   I get headaches (and I often have a headache even after the stressful thing).

e.   I feel dizzy.

f.   I feel my heart is racing or extra loud.

g.   I need to go to the toilet more often (this might be for bladder or bowels).

h.   I feel sweaty but cold.

i.   My hands or fingers are a bit shaky.

j.   I can't sit still – I need to keep moving about.

k.   I often have a breakout of spots.

l.   I feel I can't take a full breath in.

m.   I notice my breathing is faster than usual.

n.   I can't sleep well – I take ages to get to sleep or I wake up much too early.

o.   Sometimes people tell me I look very stressed even when I didn't think I had a particular facial expression.

p.   I sometimes have a panic attack. (I will talk about this more on page 47 but this is when you feel so panicky that you genuinely feel that you will die. You won't: it's caused by adrenalin and adrenalin is life-saving, not life-threatening!)

Remember, these are all normal responses to anxiety (which you'll learn more about in Part Two) and different people experience different groups of symptoms. Before we look at what your answers mean, let's look at your mental responses to anxiety. Remember, your brain is part of your body and incredibly closely connected to it.

QUIZ 3: HOW DOES YOUR MIND REACT TO ANXIETY?

The previous quiz looked at physical symptoms that people often have when they are facing a worrying or stressful situation such as an exam, performance or social event. Now think about what goes on in your mind at those times. Which of these mental reactions do you experience when you are worrying about something?

a. I can't switch my thoughts off to go to sleep.

b. I can't relax – I keep thinking of things I have to do.

c. I am more snappy – people irritate me more.

d. My thoughts are more negative.

e. Negative thoughts go round and round – I keep coming back to the same thing and I can't get it out of my head.

f. Sometimes I find myself thinking of the absolute worst thing that can happen and I kind of live through it, even though it's just in my mind – it's like a horrible story or nightmare playing out in my head and can make me really upset.

g. When one worry comes, it seems to trigger lots of completely different worries – I get into a worry phase.

h. I find it hard to concentrate on my work or on what people are saying to me.

i. I forget things easily or make mistakes.

j. My dreams are extra weird or horrible.

k. I sometimes think I'm going mad and no one else has these worries.

WHAT YOUR ANSWERS MEAN

Every one of those physical and mental symptoms is a natural and common response to a worrying event or thought. You are not alone, I promise. Even if you experience something not on that list, you are not the only one. However, even though these are completely natural and common reactions, it's important to have some control over them so that they don't overwhelm you. *Identifying* your responses to anxiety is a great start and this book will give you much more in the way of strategies. You can't really deal with something unless you see it in the correct context: in this case, the context of an anxious mind, not an ill one. This is the best news: strategies to reduce your response to anxiety help ALL the symptoms, not just one or two!

SOME THINGS TO THINK ABOUT

*★ Although anyone might experience some of these signs of anxiety, if you experience a lot of them a lot of the time, it will be exhausting and affect how you perform, feel or behave. Your life might feel dominated by these uncomfortable symptoms. You will find lots of things to help in this book.

*★ This book will show you how to deal with and reduce all these unpleasant physical and mental feelings.

*★ If you have a particular repeated physical symptom – such as stomach-aches, headaches, nausea or dizziness – it is definitely important to get it checked out by a doctor, in case it is connected to something else. (It usually isn't.)

*★ Everything on each list will benefit from any of the Instant Actions on pages 77–92. But some of the symptoms will benefit especially from carefully selected strategies. In Part Three, you will find some strategies signposted as being particularly helpful for specific symptoms, for example sleep problems, social anxiety, negative thinking and fears of public speaking.

A FEW OTHER IMPORTANT THINGS ABOUT YOU

There are many factors that go towards making you the individual that you are. These factors change as you go through life and if you can learn to identify them, it can help you manage your anxiety. Sometimes you have a bit of control over them and sometimes you don't. When you don't, knowing this helps you not to blame yourself, but when you *can* do something about the situation it's very empowering. Here are some things to be aware of.

THE PEOPLE AROUND YOU

We all live surrounded by people – some of us more so than others. In your home, there'll be one or more adults and maybe siblings or step-siblings. If you're at school, there are people your age, some of whom you like and others you don't, as well as teachers and younger or older students. If you do out-of-school activities, such as drama or sport, you'll be around people of various ages. You probably have other relatives and people connected to you – grandparents, aunts and uncles, cousins and family friends. You see hundreds of other people on social media or in the news or in television dramas or films. You also interact with strangers in shops, on transport, online.

The people around us affect us. When we see people being anxious, stressed, sad, excited, happy, angry, scared, some of these feelings rub off on us and change our thoughts and feelings. And the closer those people are to us – physically or emotionally – the stronger the effect.

I call this the "cabin crew effect". Have you ever been on an aeroplane when there's some turbulence? Most people find this stressful and we look at the cabin crew to see how they're responding. If they are carrying on their business, still smiling and looking relaxed, we immediately feel better. If they look worried, we worry more. The adults around you – in your home, in schools and public places, and through online media – are the cabin crew: if they're all behaving anxiously, it affects you. During difficult times, such as during a pandemic, economic crisis or war, adults need to remember this.

Who do you spend your time with? How do they behave in terms of anxiety and stress? Do you think sometimes their anxiety makes yours worse? Do you think that you are copying any of their negative behaviours?

I am not blaming anyone here: the people around you might have tough situations they're reacting to, or they haven't read this book and learnt how to manage anxiety. They may not realise the effect their words or actions are having, sometimes because their minds are just too full of whatever they're dealing with. What I want you to do is simply to think about:

✳ Who are your best role models? Out of your friends, family and teachers, which ones seem to deal with problems calmly and practically? Would you like to learn from them? Try to spend time with these people and let their calm and practical behaviours guide you. (I would like adults to think about themselves as role models and do their best to be good ones. I know it's not easy, though.)

✳ Are there people who make you feel more anxious? It's not your responsibility to manage other people's behaviour, but would you benefit from sometimes keeping out of their way and having your own space? I am not suggesting you avoid such people if they are close to you and they need you and you need them, but do be aware that their problems and moods will affect you. Make sure you balance this with plenty of time with positive influences and doing positive activities for *you*.

In Part Three you will find strategies but for now I'd just like you to recognise that the people around you do make a difference. They can't help it (though they will benefit from reading this book!), but the important thing is to realise that if you are surrounded by people suffering from anxiety, your own anxiety is likely to be a bit worse. That means it will be harder for you to have the great relationship with your anxiety guard dog that I want to help you to have.

Not impossible – just harder!

THINGS HAPPENING AROUND YOU

If you are going through some difficult things at the moment, this will obviously add to your anxiety. I asked you about this in Question 8 in the quiz on page 16. There are life events which anyone would find difficult. Sometimes they are just difficult periods to get through, but they may make you generally more anxious while they are happening. So, you could have one *big* thing to worry about but this could make you feel anxious about lots of other things.

If you are dealing with any of the following right now, be extra kind to yourself and don't be surprised if you find yourself with completely different and unconnected anxieties, too.

* Bereavement and grief.
* A break-up between your parents or carers.
* Someone close to you being very ill, mentally or physically.
* You being ill mentally or physically.
* Breaking up with a friend.
* A very big problem for your family, such as struggling to pay bills or a parent or carer losing a job.
* Bullying, including online.

★ Moving house when you don't want to.

★ Starting a new school, especially when you don't know anyone there.

Whatever you are going through, make sure a trusted adult knows what you're dealing with. Some of those things do need special help and the important thing is to know that help is out there: expert help that really works, with people who specialise in a particular problem and who will hear you and know what to say. You'll find some suggestions in the Resources section at the end of the book.

Do not suffer alone. Suffering alone is not good for anxiety.

ADVERSE CHILDHOOD EXPERIENCES (ACEs)

"Adverse childhood experiences" or ACEs describe very negative events that some people suffer when they are young. The evidence is that the more of these events you experience as a baby or child, the more chance that you *might* have some long-term negative effects, including increased anxiety.

ACEs include two main types of experience:

★ Things that happen directly to you – for example, losing a parent or carer; your parent or carer being too ill to look after you well; being bullied or abused.

★ Things that happen around you – for example, witnessing violence in your home; your household suffering poverty; parents or carers often being drunk or using drugs.

ACEs all share one feature: they can reduce the feeling of security that all babies and young children most need. When you're a baby or child, it's essential that an adult (one or more) cares for you in a way that makes you feel protected and then helps you start to become independent *gradually*, as you become old enough to learn to do things for yourself.

It's important to know that ACEs do not *always* cause later problems. It's just that those bad experiences can make it *harder* for you to feel confident and secure, and make you more likely to be generally anxious.

But if you have good support from other adults and good friendships as you go through school and beyond, you can still grow up strong, confident and bold. This book will help you!

The point is that when you recognise that you have suffered some difficult experiences which might affect your anxiety levels now, you can be kinder to yourself and not beat yourself up if you get more anxious and stressed than some of your friends.

I don't suggest that you just lie down and let anxiety take over, just because it might be caused by things in the past and outside your control. Knowing your vulnerability is a very good start to becoming stronger. When you know *why* something is happening, you can take steps to deal with it.

So, even if you have been unlucky enough to have experienced very negative events as a child, there are things you and the adults who support you can do now to help you have good well-being. Anxiety is not a fixed and physical part of you like the colour of your eyes: it's just how your brain makes you feel in certain situations. And you can train your brain to do it differently, just as you can train your brain to be better at any skill.

MOVING FORWARD

You now know a bit more about yourself and your relationship with anxiety. You might even have started to feel more relaxed and to realise that everyone is anxious sometimes: it does not mean there is something wrong with you. Anxiety feels unpleasant, but there's so much you're going to learn about how to make it feel better and how to manage it so that it does its job without dominating you.

What would it feel like if you could manage anxiety better? Which of these things would you love to aim for and achieve?

* I would not keep having a feeling of dread when I haven't even got something scary coming up.
* I would be able to think of a worrying thing without feeling overwhelmed by it.
* Life would not seem full of things to fear.
* Worries would not keep going round and round in my head.
* I would feel more positive about life.
* I would feel more confident and in control.
* I would be able to switch off and enjoy relaxing times such as holidays.
* I would be able to focus on the things I want or need to focus on.
* My mind would not constantly be taken up with "what ifs".
* I would find it easier to fall asleep at night.
* When I get anxious about something, I would have techniques to manage well.

Let's do this!

PART TWO
ALL ABOUT ANXIETY

I'd love you to understand exactly what anxiety is. If anxiety has a job, what is it? What is the point of it? (There's almost always a point in the things our brains and bodies do.) I'll share facts and truths. Only then will the strategies in Part Three make the best sense and only then will you feel confident in them. I want you to use the strategies with that confidence, otherwise you're just doing what I tell you, rather than doing what you *know* has a good reason behind it.

WHAT EXACTLY IS ANXIETY?

Anxiety is a feeling of worry, fear, dread or nervousness. The initial feeling of anxiety, or the "stress response", is caused by the chemical reactions in a system in your brain called the "sympathetic nervous system". ("Sympathetic" literally means "suffering with" and here it just means that a set of reactions happen together and create a range of responses in your body.)

These reactions happen when the body's stress response is activated because the brain believes there's a threat or problem to deal with. The threat could be an external physical threat, such as fire or someone holding a knife. Or it could be in your mind, such as thinking about an exam or performance. (This is still real, in the sense of being genuine and important, but it's mental, not physical.) Or it could be something which probably isn't *actually* dangerous but which your brain *interprets* as dangerous, such as a large spider or walking across a high bridge.

It could be something big, such as facing a worrying medical procedure or an important exam. Or something smaller, such as needing to ask a question in public. Or smaller still, such as meeting a new person. And each of us will have different opinions about what is big and what is small. For example, different people will have different levels of anxiety about answering a question in class or walking into a room full of strangers or seeing a spider.

The brain interprets all these very different threats identically at first, because the response happens before the brain has a chance to analyse the possible danger. The brain simply goes "threat – action", more quickly than you could even say those words, and triggers a chemical response throughout the body. Only then can the thinking part of your brain start working out what to do and how worrying the threat actually is. Or isn't.

A really good illustration of this is when you jump, flinch or even scream when a loud noise happens. Your brain instantly reacts to the noise as a threat. Then, almost immediately afterwards, the thinking part of your brain processes that it was just a door banging – or whatever – and you start to relax.

THE PARASYMPATHETIC NERVOUS SYSTEM

"Para" means "alongside" – think of parallel lines. The sympathetic nervous system activates various processes in the body during stress; the parasympathetic nervous system tells those processes to stand down, when the stress is over. So, the parasympathetic system allows your heart, breathing, digestive system, temperature control and hormone levels all to return to relaxed mode. It pulls everything gently back to balance.

WHAT ARE THESE CHEMICAL REACTIONS?

Deep in your brain, a part called the amygdala sends a message to another part, the hypothalamus. This sends an instant message to the adrenal glands (in your kidneys) to release adrenalin. Adrenalin and cortisol race round your body with the following immediate effects:

* Heart rate and breathing speed up – so blood goes more quickly around your body, taking oxygen and glucose (energy) to your large muscles in case you need to run (flight) or defend yourself (fight) or freeze.

  Note: adrenalin is sometimes called epinephrin and they are sometimes spelt "adrenaline" and "epinephrine".

* Your attention is fully on whatever the threat is – and you might not be aware of other, more irrelevant, things going on around you.

You might notice some other physical things, too:

* Feeling cold – because the blood is diverted away from your skin towards your muscles.
* Not wanting to eat – because the reaction slows your digestion.
* Needing to go to the toilet.
* Feeling dizzy.
* Finding it hard to sit still – you want to get up and you might pace around.
* Shaky hands or legs – you might particularly notice this if you are standing up to give a speech, for example.

All of these things happen as your sympathetic nervous system is activated. You might not notice them straightaway if you are too busy dealing with the situation. Sometimes people don't even notice pain when they are having this anxiety response.

It's not a comfortable feeling. It's not supposed to be

comfortable, because your brain does not want you to relax right now. If you relaxed, you wouldn't get yourself out of the danger your brain believes it has detected!

BEWARE THE DELAYED REACTION

I mentioned during the introduction that while writing this book I have been going through a very distressing time of worry in my close family. When I wrote those words, I was coping, managing the anxiety and staying outwardly strong, but very worried inside. The situation improved and, on a scale of zero to ten, the worry reduced from ten to four. Maybe three.

A couple of days later, I had what I describe as an emotional crash. Out of the blue and for no immediate reason, I became overwhelmed with emotion, couldn't stop crying and felt that I couldn't breathe. I got the breathing under control using one of the techniques I talk about in Part Three, and I cancelled everything I was meant to be doing that day and just took it easy. I allowed myself to think through everything that had happened, accepted my reactions as perfectly natural, and looked after myself a bit better.

That was not an anxiety attack but it is what can happen after a stressful time, if you hold too much tension and anxiety inside you. But sometimes you don't have a choice, because the things happening around you are too much to deal with at that time. So when a delayed reaction like this happens, it's important to recognise it as natural, normal, human. It's also worth noting that this was the third time in under three years that I'd gone through something similar. I was carrying a lot of anxiety, without letting it go.

No one is superman or superwoman. However strong you are, you sometimes crack. The strongest trees bend in the wind – they don't stand rigid, they allow the wind to sway them. And if you try to be so strong that you don't bend, you'll crack and break.

It has helped me to go through this because I can look after myself better now, and be even better at helping other people, including you. Although I had that emotional crash and felt terrible, I was not ill with anxiety and I was able to recover just by doing the self-help strategies in this book. But I did keep an eye on myself and, if the self-help hadn't worked, after a while I would have sought professional help.

You'll find strategies for such delayed reactions on pages 94–5.

WHAT IS THE DIFFERENCE BETWEEN ANXIETY AND STRESS?

Anxiety and stress are extremely similar and tightly connected. Often, you can use either word interchangeably. But when you look closely, they are not exactly the same.

Biologically, anxiety and stress both describe ways in which our brain, body and mind react to a perceived threat. As you've already discovered, when the brain detects a threat it triggers an instant response to make us ready for whatever action might be needed. And that response includes physical and mental aspects.

You can think of "stress" as being the physical responses and "anxiety" being the mental responses.

The physical responses usually appear first and instantly – the heart rate and breathing speeding up, muscles tensing. The mental responses come just afterwards – worrying, thinking, analysing, feeling. For example, imagine you see someone come towards you: your heart rate speeds and your muscles tense, and *then* you start to think "What's happening? Is this a danger to me? Should I run or scream?" The physical response came first.

Sometimes the mental response comes first. For example, imagine you suddenly think about a test or performance that's coming up: that anxious thought triggers the physical responses of sweating, breathing faster and heart racing.

While you are feeling anxious, your worries are also triggering more stress response. So stress and anxiety become linked in a circle, one feeding the other. They become hard to separate – we can describe them differently but they're all part of the same set of experiences.

Some people might experience or notice the physical symptoms more and describe themselves as "stressed" and others might experience or notice the mental symptoms more and describe themselves as "anxious". But in reality both sets of people are experiencing physical and mental symptoms – they are just more aware of and affected by some symptoms than others. That's OK. And it's useful, because being aware of what's going on in our body and mind allows us to start to have some power over them.

You can now see that there is a difference between stress and anxiety but that they are very closely linked. They both begin in the brain; they are both natural responses to threat; they are both useful because they raise your alert level so that you can deal with whatever the situation is. Although they are both natural and useful, they can both be a problem when we have too much of them or we don't take certain steps to manage them.

Even though this book is technically about anxiety, because the two things are so connected, it is also very much about stress. You will learn to deal with both types of symptom.

WHAT BENEFITS DOES ANXIETY GIVE US?

Super-performance! If you're anxious before a race, you'll run faster than if you're super-relaxed. If you're anxious before an audition or performance, you'll focus really well and have the best chance of success. If you're nervous before answering a question in public, you'll concentrate on your answer.

This is because of how the stress response has evolved over many thousands of years. Let me explain.

Our brains are very similar to how they were hundreds of thousands of years ago when our early human ancestors wandered the plains of Africa. Then, the threats were from things like lions, snakes and strangers. Humans who reacted fast and strongly to those dangers were more likely to survive, so the stress response was a survival tool. (Other animals have the same stress response, with each species evolving to react to the dangers it faced.)

Even though the threats have mostly changed over the centuries, the stress response hasn't because the stress response works for all dangers. And, anyway, the threats are not completely different: we still ought to be alert when we see possibly dangerous animals, potential enemies or any situation that threatens our security, including mental security. For example, we naturally feel wary when we meet a stranger: it's not exactly that we think they might be dangerous, but we still have to work out whether they are friend or enemy and it makes sense to assume briefly that they might be an enemy. Just in case.

And the stress response has to be super-quick, as a precaution. It has to react more quickly than we can think about things, because our thoughts are relatively slow – still fast, but slow relative to the anxiety response.

What this means is that because the stress response is there to make you run fast enough to escape a lion or fight well enough to beat an enemy, it gives you huge powers, physical and mental. So, you are likely to give your best performance in a race, competition, exam, performance, audition or interview that you feel anxious about.

Your anxiety about the challenge is what gives you the power to succeed. Your anxiety is your superpower!

TIMES WHEN IT'S USEFUL TO FEEL ANXIOUS

Here are some situations when anxiety can be very useful:

*★ **When you are preparing for something difficult, important and challenging –** perhaps an exam, match, race, competition, presentation or performance.

*★ **When you are going through a worrying situation –** perhaps there's an illness going round and your anxiety makes you take sensible precautions; or you smell smoke and your anxiety makes you take steps to stay safe.

*★ **When you have a difficult decision to make and there are things in the future that you can't predict –** perhaps you have to decide the best way to deal with an awkward situation with a friend, or you need to break off a relationship, or you have to decide whether to say yes or no to an opportunity.

But even when you have one of those situations, anxiety is only useful when you can do something to help the situation. For example, just before a match or performance, anxiety will keep you alert so you can super-perform. A bit of anxiety a few months before an exam could make you get down to revision in good time. And if some anxiety about dealing with a problematic friendship is going to help you make thoughtful choices, that's no bad thing. In other words, when anxiety might make you do something better, it's welcome.

So, anxiety can keep your attention on things that are important to you, encourage you to work hard or practise your skills and passions and help you rise to the challenge and do your very best.

TIMES WHEN IT'S NOT USEFUL TO FEEL ANXIOUS

However, there are lots of times when anxiety is not helpful:

- ★ When there's nothing you can do about the situation.
- ★ When nothing bad is actually happening or likely to happen.
- ★ When you're trying to sleep.
- ★ When you're trying to relax.
- ★ When you're trying to focus on something else.
- ★ When it starts to dominate or spoil your daily life.

Even when anxiety isn't useful, it's still natural and normal and allowing it in is not always a bad thing. For example, if you're worried about something bad happening, there's nothing wrong with spending a little time going through that worry in your mind. It could prepare you in case the bad thing does happen. However, doing this too much is not helpful and is likely to stop you enjoying life to the full or focusing on the things that are more important.

WHY PEOPLE ARE DIFFERENT

You have probably already noticed or felt that some people are more anxious than others. Some people worry out loud and don't try to hide it, so you can tell when they are anxious. But don't be too sure: some people seem *not* to be worriers when they are just hiding it.

It is true, however, that people vary widely in how anxious they tend to be and how they react to difficult or worrying things in their lives.

Let's look at some of these differences and the possible causes. You'll recognise some of them because I mentioned them on pages 17, 23 and 26 when I was asking you to think about yourself and your own situation.

You can also read the real-life stories of people with different experiences with anxiety on pages 187–96 to get an idea of how everyone responds differently.

WHAT CAN MAKE SOME PEOPLE NATURALLY MORE ANXIOUS THAN OTHERS?

When I say "naturally", I don't necessarily mean how people are born or how their "nature" is. We usually can't tell whether a particular behaviour comes from biological make-up or has been shaped by someone's environment. But some people do seem to be generally more anxious and vulnerable to suffering from anxiety than others. Here are some possible explanations:

* **Genes –** the genetic code we inherit from our biological parents is very complicated and there is no single "gene for anxiety", but it is possible that genes play a part in anxiety levels. There's a lot of disagreement about this, though, and it's hard to measure. Note, too, that even if you inherit genes "for" anxiety, you will not necessarily be anxious. But you are more likely to be.

* **Who we spend time with –** we tend to copy those around us, even if we aren't aware we're doing so. Anxious people raise the stress levels of those around them. (You saw this on page 23.) They don't mean to but it's just what tends to happen. So, if you have a parent or carer who is very anxious, this could make you more anxious.

* **Adverse Childhood Experiences (ACEs) –** you learnt about these on page 26. When very bad things have happened in your earlier life it *might* make you more prone to suffering anxiety and finding it hard to stop worrying when you don't need to worry.

* **Personality traits –** there are aspects of personality that

can make it more likely that you feel anxious about things that some other people take in their stride.

Let's look at some of these personality traits now. It's very helpful to build a picture of what kind of characteristics you have as these can make a difference to how you react to anxiety in your life.

NEUROTICISM

Neurotic literally means nervous and when psychologists measure neuroticism they look at how emotional your responses are to things that happen around you. A highly neurotic person is likely to have relatively intense and negative reactions to events. A less neurotic person finds it easier to keep things in perspective and not react so strongly to negative things. They might look calmer than the more neurotic person. Or they might keep their feelings hidden.

Remember that reacting to a perceived threat is not a bad thing. But being highly neurotic does make you more vulnerable to anxiety, so it's helpful to know if this is a part of your personal make-up.

If you score highly on neuroticism, you may have mood swings and find yourself feeling sad or anxious more often than someone scoring low on this trait. You may tend to ruminate, or overthink, and to catastrophise, or imagine worst-case scenarios.

Neuroticism is one of the "big five" personality traits that most experts believe are more or less fixed throughout our lives. We can, however, learn to alter how we react to them, especially when we have a good understanding of how they affect us. You can find free online tests that will give you a rough idea of your level of neuroticism. It's a good idea to do more than one test as the results may vary. Try this test.

QUIZ: LOOK AT YOUR NEUROTICISM

Below are ten statements for you to think about. How many of them strongly describe you? This will give you a general idea of how neurotic you might be. The more of them you feel describe you, and the more strongly you feel this, the higher you are likely to score on neuroticism. (But remember: this test has only a few statements so it can only give you a broad picture, not the detail of your level of neuroticism.)

1. I usually expect the worst.
2. When a person says something I find upsetting, I can't let it go easily.
3. I find it very hard to relax, even at weekends and on holiday.
4. I would like to change a lot about my character.
5. I panic under pressure.
6. I often feel I'm being judged and that feels threatening.
7. I am often really irritated by other people.
8. My moods change very quickly.
9. I easily lose control and say things I regret.
10. I would say I'm a big worrier.

In the Resources, you'll find pointers towards learning more about neuroticism and other personality traits.

Important: saying those things might have made you feel bad about yourself so please now say some positive things about yourself. In your head – or out loud – finish these sentences:

Something I'm proud of is…
The best thing about me is…
I love to remember the time when I…
I am grateful that…
I feel happy when…

TYPE A PERSONALITY

We can talk about people as being Type A or Type B personalities, and this can affect anxiety, with Type A people tending to experience higher levels. You might be strongly one or the other or you might be very much in the middle.

Type A people are in a hurry, competitive and ambitious. They are often highly stressed because they push themselves hard and it matters very much to them whether they do well at everything. They take things seriously and don't mess about when they're trying to achieve their goals. They get frustrated by people messing around.

Type B people are typically more relaxed, patient and easily satisfied with whatever they achieve. They might know what they want but they are happy to take their time getting there. If they have a deadline, they pace themselves rather than starting immediately. They like to play and have fun and don't always take things very seriously.

You might find that you are Type A in certain types of situations and more Type B in other situations. Lots of people are not strongly A or B but a mixture.

QUIZ: ARE YOU MORE TYPE A OR TYPE B?

Look at these two sets of statements and see how many you strongly identify with from each list.

If you are a Type A person you will identify with many of these statements:

★ I am ambitious and set myself high standards.

★ I take on a lot of work and often take on responsibilities like leading or organising.

★ I want to get things done quickly – it annoys me when people move slowly.

★ If I have a deadline, I don't wait until the last minute but get the work done as soon as possible.

★ Winning and getting top grades is very important to me – I feel bad when I don't achieve this.

★ I get impatient when people mess around.

★ I get stressed about things because it's so important that I do well and the thought of failure or messing up is a really big deal for me.

★ I don't take a break until all my work is done.

★ When I've finished my work, I start something else as I feel guilty if I'm not doing anything.

If you are a Type B person you will identify with many of these statements:

★ I'm not competitive – of course winning is a great feeling, but it's not the point.

★ I like joining in activities even if I'm not brilliant at them – it's just fun to join in and, you never know, I might be good at it.

- ⭐ I don't take things too seriously – it's best to have a laugh in life.

- ⭐ I don't worry much about things that are a way off or might not happen.

- ⭐ I wait until close to the deadline before I start a task – no point in working hard until you have to.

- ⭐ People would describe me as a pretty laid-back person.

- ⭐ When I've finished a piece of work, I go and relax – I deserve it.

- ⭐ I find it easy to switch off.

Neither type is "better" than the other. There are advantages to both. But when we're thinking about anxiety, it's important to know that if you're more of a Type A person, the likelihood is you'll be more anxious. You are more vulnerable to suffering the downsides of anxiety and it's likely to get in the way of you enjoying your life.

Therefore, Type A people need to take a few more steps to manage their anxiety so that it doesn't become a problem.

CAN WE BECOME LESS ANXIOUS OR IS IT A FIXED PERSONALITY TRAIT?

To some extent, some people just are more anxious than others. It's linked to more or less fixed aspects of their personality, genes and experiences. However, how anxious you feel at the moment will not stay the same all your life. It is in your power – and this book will help you – to suffer less from anxiety as you go through your life. Let me explain and give you three reassuring truths:

1. **Anxiety levels change as events change**

   We can't usually affect the things that are going on around us. At the moment you might have some difficult things to deal with: those will change. I obviously can't tell you how and when, but they will. You will have calmer times in your life and if you recognise those calmer times and use them to heal your anxious mind, you'll be less anxious for a while. How you feel is how you feel *right now*. So, you won't always feel this anxious. But the next two points are even more important.

2. **You can learn strategies to manage your anxiety and reduce it**

   Even though aspects of your personality might not change much, you *can* change how you react and behave when that personality makes you suffer anxiety. Everyone, including the most anxious and those who've had the most challenging experiences, can learn strategies to reduce the effects of anxiety. That's what Part Three will teach you. So, even if anxiety feels like a big and scary enemy for you right now, the skills you'll learn will allow you to feel safe from it and handle it with strength, resilience and courage. It is a part of you but you can learn to control it and to enjoy your life just as much as anyone else. This is about training that guard dog and learning to live happily alongside it.

3. **As you grow older, you can learn from your experiences and respond more positively to anxiety**

   The more experiences you have – especially the challenging, difficult and unpleasant ones – the more you can develop your ability to cope with anxiety. Not all adults do learn from their experiences: some just keep on fighting with their guard dog instead of training it and working with it. But with good advice and support – which is exactly what *No Worries* is giving you – you can become a person who does learn from experiences. And you don't have to wait until you're an adult! When you read the real-life experiences starting on page 187, you will see that many of the adults have learnt useful skills from their experiences, but some still struggle. Perhaps they could have benefited from a book like this when they were younger! I will show you that you have already learnt so much from whatever you have been through. Whether it's something big like the pandemic or losing someone you loved, to something smaller like worrying about a test or a situation with a friendship, I can show you how to let your experiences shape you positively, so that, even if you have an anxious personality, the anxiety is only a small part of it. You are so very much more than your worries!

WHEN IS ANXIETY A PROBLEM?

You might be reading this book because you feel that anxiety is a problem for you. You might be worried that it's going to cause you physical damage. You might even be worrying about heart attacks or other serious illnesses. If you sometimes have panic attacks you might feel this very strongly when they are happening.

I want to set your mind at rest and let you know just how anxiety can affect your health and how it can't.

Let's not worry about worry or have anxiety about anxiety!

The next few pages will answer some of your questions and worries about anxiety. I'll also go over some of the real problems that people can suffer when their anxiety is too much. If you identify with these problems, Part Three will point you towards strategies for self-help and also towards professional help if you need it. But you might not need it because for many (most) people, healthy strategies and life skills are enough.

GENTLE BUT IMPORTANT WARNING

Thinking or reading about negative or worrying things is likely to raise your anxiety and may lower your mood. This is even more likely if you are going through an anxious phase at the moment. The next few pages will focus on negative or worrying things so you might feel more anxious for a few minutes. However, it's still a very good idea to read them, even if they make you feel distressed. Anxiety is not something to run away from; it cannot hurt you. It's your guard dog, remember, and you are learning to tame it so it works brilliantly for you. You do not train dogs by running from them. In fact, running from a dog usually makes it more likely to attack. Part Three will teach you not to run away from or try to avoid the things that worry you.

So, yes, I am giving you a "trigger warning": you might feel your anxiety levels rise while you read the next few pages. But I am asking you to put on your bravest face and read the pages anyway.

These pages will not harm you. They are your second step to being able to control your anxiety. (The first step was choosing to read this book.)

If you do feel more anxious while reading, the best thing you can do is jump to pages 77–92, do one of the Instant Actions for a few minutes and then come back to finish reading this section when you're ready. You will be ready.

CAN TOO MUCH ANXIETY EVER MAKE ME ILL?

If you feel too anxious too often, or if you very often feel anxious about things that you don't really need to feel anxious about, this can begin to dominate your life. When your anxiety becomes more than you can control, you can develop an anxiety disorder, or your general health can be affected in various ways that can make it harder to succeed in some areas of your life.

People often talk about "suffering from anxiety". This can mean two different things. It might mean that someone has been diagnosed with an anxiety disorder: they have a specific reaction to anxiety which requires some treatment to make it better. Or it might mean more generally that someone feels more anxious than they are comfortable with and it is spoiling their life to some extent. In that case, they can also be helped by a health professional, even if a doctor might not diagnose an actual anxiety disorder.

Each anxiety disorder has a list of particular symptoms and only a trained person can decide whether you have an anxiety disorder or general anxiety.

Anxiety disorders are unpleasant but there are good treatments so that people can either improve and be cured, or learn strategies to make their condition more manageable so they can enjoy a happy and successful life.

I'll talk about some specific anxiety problems in the next pages.

PANIC ATTACKS

Many people never suffer panic attacks, though they might sometimes feel panicky. Some people suffer one attack and never experience it again. Some suffer them quite often. Sometimes it's clear that a particular stressful situation or thought has triggered it. Sometimes it just seems to happen out of the blue with no obvious reason.

A panic attack is when you suddenly experience several of the following signs:

*★ Racing heart – you might be able to feel palpitations or hear pounding in your ears.

*★ Dizziness or faintness.

- Feeling you can't breathe.
- Feeling of choking.
- Nausea.
- Feeling of unreality.
- Thinking you're going mad.
- Thinking you're dying.
- Extreme fear and discomfort.
- Feeling very cold or hot.
- A desperate need to escape.

The attack might disappear very quickly or last for a few minutes. It won't last longer than that.

The physical feeling of a panic attack is so intense that you might be desperate to escape the situation, perhaps by running from the room. Or you might just be very shaky, sweaty and terrified of what is happening to you. You might be unable to do whatever you are meant to be doing, such as giving a speech or facing an exam. You are completely focused on the intensity of the feelings in your body.

Your panic attack is caused by one natural chemical: adrenalin. You've met it already – it's one of the stress response hormones. It's released in your body quite harmlessly many times a day, but occasionally your body produces too much and the effects are quick – but temporary. It will stop. Your body is only capable of producing adrenalin for a short time before it has to stop, even if you do nothing about it.

A panic attack is a horrible experience and you might think you're going to die. The first thing I must tell you – so that you can tell yourself – is that you're not. You're not. You only think you are because your heart is racing so much that you think you must be about to have a heart attack. This is caused by the adrenalin which your body is overproducing. The amount of adrenalin your body is capable of producing cannot kill you. (You might be interested to know that adrenalin is what some people with allergies carry with them to save their lives when they have a severe allergic reaction. It's life-saving!)

Panic is just an exaggerated stress response. Your brain has made an annoying mistake in releasing so much adrenalin for so little reason. Your guard dog has become overexcited and is racing round barking at nothing, or almost nothing. But soon the guard dog will exhaust itself and go back to its kennel. The symptoms of panic are temporary: your body cannot keep making more adrenalin, so very soon your heart rate and breathing will return to normal. Even if you don't do anything about it.

Panic doesn't feel nice but it will not harm you, just upset you. "This will not harm me" is something to remember any time you feel panic.

You will find strategies for dealing with panic attacks in Part Three. Go straight to page 92 if you wish.

WORRY CHAINS AND ANXIETY SPIRALS

Once your brain has been triggered to worry about something, you might then start worrying about other things that you hadn't been thinking about. I call this a worry chain. It's as though the worries are all linked together and when you rattle one link the whole chain rattles. This happens because worry is a feeling and when you trigger the feeling of worry, anything can become worrying.

An anxiety spiral is similar. It describes how sometimes, in some people, a worry starts and then they are dragged into a whole load of worrying thoughts that just get worse and worse or stronger and stronger.

Do either or both of those feel familiar to you? If not, you're lucky as you're probably not badly affected by anxiety. But if they do feel familiar, don't worry: there's nothing wrong with you. Your brain has just developed a habit of allowing itself to be pulled into worrying chains of thoughts. Just noticing these thought patterns is helpful because then you can take steps to put a good strategy in place. You will feel and cope much better when you've learnt some strategies in Part Three.

PHOBIAS

A phobia is an extreme fear of something, a fear which causes huge anxiety for the person even when they aren't actually facing the thing. We are all afraid of some things and for good reason, because some things are dangerous – or were dangerous to early humans – and being afraid of them is healthy. But some people either have a strong fear of something that isn't truly dangerous (such as the colour yellow or having blood taken), or they are afraid of something that could be dangerous but their fear dominates their life even when the dangerous thing is nowhere near (such as being afraid of fire when there is no fire or risk of fire).

But a phobia is not simply a strong fear or hatred of something. It is classed as a true phobia when the fear or hatred leads the sufferer to change aspects of their life to avoid something, in a way that is out of proportion to the real threat. For example, someone with a phobia of spiders will obsessively check the room for them before sitting down or will avoid a place where they once saw a spider; someone with a phobia of flying might travel huge extra distances by car – or never have a foreign holiday; someone with a fear of heights might walk a longer route to avoid a bridge. And when the sufferer has to face their fears they will be extremely stressed, sweaty, shaky, panicky.

Phobias spoil people's enjoyment of life and even, sometimes, their ability to succeed.

Some well-known phobias include:

- ⭐ Agoraphobia – open spaces.
- ⭐ Claustrophobia – enclosed spaces.
- ⭐ Emetophobia – vomiting.
- ⭐ Mysophobia – disease or germs.
- ⭐ Social phobia – people and social situations (see page 56).
- ⭐ Trypanophobia – needles.
- ⭐ Ophidiophobia – snakes.

People often say they have a phobia of something when what they really mean is they strongly hate or fear it but their life is not badly affected by their fear. Of course, if you wish to, you can say "I'm a bit phobic about XYZ", but don't confuse this with someone who really is suffering a phobia that dominates their life.

If you feel you are suffering a phobia that is affecting your life, do seek help. It really is worth it. Treatment usually involves helping you very gradually feel better when you face the thing you fear. Avoiding it is almost never the solution. Part Three will give you more details about this.

It's possible to have a phobia about almost anything. Here are some less common but well-recognised things that some people have a phobia about: pumpkin seeds, balloons, holes, chickens. The fact that your phobia is about one of these less common things doesn't make it easier to deal with, as you might find that people don't take you seriously or don't understand. It can be very difficult to avoid these items, too.

There's even a word for the fear of very long words. It's presumably very rare but if you have a fear of very long words, don't turn away but take a few calm, slow breaths before you read on. Ready? The word is "hippopotomonstrosesquipedaliophobia".

No, me neither. I'm not afraid of it but it is ridiculously long.

Sometimes a phobia stems from a bad experience as a child or even someone accidentally planting a fear in you at a vulnerable age. But most often we can't be sure why someone has developed a phobia.

What we do know is that it's a form of anxiety. Your anxiety, instead of being general, is focused strongly on this one thing. You are also likely to find that when you're generally feeling anxious, your phobia may feel worse.

Even if you don't have one of these phobias, I hope you can start to imagine how difficult life might be for someone who has a phobia about something that is difficult to avoid. If you or someone you know suffers from a phobia, first see the strategies on page 138. If that isn't enough, then do seek help, first through your family doctor. It's one of the easiest types of anxiety disorders to treat but it is hard to deal with it yourself.

SCHOOL REFUSAL, SCHOOL ANXIETY OR SCHOOL PHOBIA

I didn't include this in the list of phobias because it's a little different. If you are one of those people who finds going to school unbearably difficult and you feel that you absolutely cannot attend, it's not *exactly* that you are afraid of school itself. Your anxiety may be connected to some aspect of the school experience: it could be a social phobia or anxiety around people; it could be some bullying or problem behaviour that happens to you at school; it could be a fear of failure (kakorrhaphiophobia!) that you feel when you're there; it could be a fear of leaving the house or of something happening to your family. It could be a combination of things that worry you. And it could be something that you can't even explain.

It could be that the physical symptoms of discomfort that you associate with going to school or with something that happens at school are sometimes so strong that you feel unable to cope with them. You might also have panic attacks when faced with going to school; or it could be that you had a panic attack once at school and you are afraid to repeat the experience. Your adults should look at what exactly it is you're anxious about when you feel unable to go to school.

Of course, if something like bullying or any other specific negative situation is happening, that needs to be sorted. Ask an adult for their help with this. But otherwise we need to find a way for you to manage the anxiety symptoms so that they stop being a problem for you. The strategies in Part Three will be a great start.

What we do know is that avoiding the thing we are so afraid of is almost never the way to deal with fear. This just *increases* our anxiety. Avoidance is called a "negative coping strategy", as you'll learn on page 60. At the time, it helps you cope but it has negative results: you still can't face the source of your anxiety and you let your life become less good as you keep avoiding something which would help you have a better life. Also, it reinforces your belief that you can't handle something and that makes it harder the next time and more likely that you'll avoid it again.

OBSESSIVE COMPULSIVE DISORDER (OCD)

Nowadays, people too often say "I'm a bit OCD about that". It's like saying "I'm a bit phobic" and it's annoying and undermining for people who *do* suffer from these diagnosed conditions. Yes, it is possible to have a milder or a stronger phobia and it is possible to have a milder or stronger version of OCD. But it is important to recognise the difference between "being a bit OCD" and having actual obsessive compulsive disorder. People with OCD (or a phobia) have some really big challenges just to get through every day.

The best-known form of OCD involves obsessive hand-washing and avoidance of germs. But lots of people experience OCD differently, without the focus on cleanliness. They might have obsessive intrusive thoughts and carry out routines to "protect" themselves from their negative thoughts. People like this have an OCD that is quite hidden and you might not know unless they tell you about it.

The one thing that is the same for all sufferers of OCD is that they are obsessively compelled to behave in certain ways, even if those ways seem illogical or odd or unnecessary to everyone else. Usually, they know themselves that their actions are illogical but they are still compelled to do them – compelled by how their mind works.

For example, they might be obsessed about even or odd numbers and not be able to leave a room without switching each switch an even or odd number of times, "in case something bad happens". Or they might have to rub their hands 33 times while washing them, or hold their breath until a phone is answered, or blink six times to make a bad thought not come true.

When I was a child, if I went to the bathroom in the night I told myself I had to get back into bed before the cistern noise stopped; it was like a little challenge. Someone with OCD might have a similar mental challenge but would be extremely anxious if they didn't manage it, whereas I would just think, "Oh well."

Lots of people who don't have OCD are obsessive checkers. I will check many times that I've locked the door or that my phone is with me; when I'm leaving the house I know I've checked everything but I'll do it again and again, wiggling the door-handle in case I've somehow not noticed that it isn't locked.

I don't have OCD – though I do think I check too much and it's borderline obsessive behaviour. What makes it not OCD is that I'm not *compelled* to take certain actions. But one thing I've noticed: when I'm feeling generally more anxious than usual, my checking reaches new heights. When I'm relaxed I don't check things more than once. So, as you learnt in the section about worry chains and anxiety spirals on page 49, when you have the emotion of worry going on in your mind, anything can become worrying. If you feel you check things unreasonably often, first see if you can manage this by slowing your thoughts down so that you can tell yourself that everything is fine and you have already checked enough. If this doesn't work and you worry you might have OCD, talk to a trusted adult, who can guide you towards help.

POST-TRAUMATIC STRESS DISORDER (PTSD)

Normally, when you experience something extremely distressing, shocking or terrifying, it takes a while for you to recover and feel OK again. Sometimes you might recover quickly and sometimes it will take longer. That's all perfectly healthy and natural. But sometimes this recovery doesn't happen and then you might remain very distressed, anxious, afraid and "traumatised" for a long time. (Traumatised literally means damaged or injured.) Then you might be diagnosed with Post-Traumatic Stress Disorder (PTSD).

A common symptom of PTSD is having vivid flashbacks to the distressing event but with the flashbacks being exaggerated. For example, in the flashback even worse things could happen than actually did. It can almost be like being in a bad dream even though you're awake. And, indeed, people with PTSD do often have very bad dreams.

PTSD can be linked to general anxiety, too. So, someone suffering PTSD might be more anxious in general. And someone who is more anxious in general might be more likely to experience PTSD. It can often be linked to panic attacks.

PTSD can be treated in various ways and responds well to talking therapies. Learning breathing and grounding techniques will be very important for dealing with the feelings of fear or panic when they occur.

If you think PTSD might apply to you, you should definitely talk to your doctor as you are likely to need some help to recover.

SOCIAL ANXIETY

Social anxiety (sometimes called social phobia) involves great
fear of and discomfort in situations involving other people. As
with OCD, lots of people identify with this because it's normal
to feel a bit anxious when meeting someone new, talking to
someone you don't know well, walking into a room of strangers
or speaking in public. You might also describe yourself as shy. But
social anxiety is much more than ordinary shyness. A diagnosis
of social anxiety only comes if you feel so much distress that it
is making ordinary daily activities difficult or impossible and you
try to avoid meeting or talking to other people.

You have heard of agoraphobia – fear of public spaces. This
is usually a form of social anxiety and sufferers avoid others by
staying at home. Agoraphobics find it terribly hard to go out.
Avoiding going out might make you feel safe, just as avoiding
talking to people might make you feel safe, but if you avoid the
things you fear you become *more* frightened of them.

Your social anxiety might focus on a particular fear: perhaps
that you will blush, or stammer, or sweat or say something
silly. Maybe you fear this because it once happened or often
happens. Or you've seen it happen to someone else. These are
very common things and the more you worry about them, the
more likely they become. You know they can't really harm you
– no one died of blushing – but it's still unpleasant for you and
the more you think about it the worse it feels. So you might be
tempted to try to avoid speaking in public.

The trouble is that you can't avoid it forever – and if you try,
you'll be missing loads of important opportunities for a great life.
So it's definitely worth dealing with and maybe asking for help.

Part Three will direct you towards good strategies and you'll
also find resources at the back of the book.

What should you do now if you believe you suffer from any
of those disorders? Continue reading this book as you will learn

even more and find some strategies that will certainly help you. But you also now have the language to describe your feelings if and when you choose to talk to a professional about them. Start by talking to a trusted adult and they can help you get in touch with your family doctor or counselling service.

HOW DOES ANXIETY AFFECT YOUR BODY AND MIND?

You've already looked at how you personally experience the effects of anxiety in your body and mind, but let's look at them more widely, so that you can understand how others might be affected. We'll also look at effects outside your body and mind.

These effects can last a short time – perhaps just while the worry is there – or can become a regular part of your life, especially if your life has a lot of worries or you are a big worrier generally. Even though none of these things is particularly dangerous, they make your life feel less good and it would certainly be useful if you could reduce their power. That's what Part Three will help with!

When you have too much anxiety or it goes on for too long, you might notice certain unpleasant, annoying or distressing effects on your body, your work and achievements, your mind and your life in general. Some of these might happen quite quickly after the triggering event but others might not show up until later.

EFFECTS ON YOUR BODY

* Problems with digestive system – stomach-aches or cramps, diarrhoea or constipation.
* Nausea – feeling sick and possibly being sick (though most people do not vomit – they just fear they will).

* Pain anywhere – particularly in the head, face and jaw, neck and shoulders.

* Clenching your jaw, which can even make your teeth hurt.

* Dizziness and lightheadedness.

* Clumsiness – dropping or breaking things.

* Voice changes – your voice might go very high or breathless; you might feel that your words stick in your throat.

* Dry mouth – and tongue sticking to the roof of your mouth.

* Losing hair.

EFFECTS ON YOUR MIND

* Low mood – feeling anxious and feeling "down" are often linked.

* Difficulty concentrating – it's hard to focus on important tasks when you're full of worry.

* Feeling that you're the only person whose mind works like this – that there's something wrong with you.

* Feeling lonely.

* Feeling frustrated with yourself.

* Negative thoughts intruding and going round and round – you can feel you're crazy for thinking like this.

* Finding it hard to fall asleep and stay asleep for the whole night; you might wake very early in the morning.

EFFECTS ON YOUR WORK OR ACHIEVEMENTS

* Poor concentration might make you perform less well on homework or tests.

* Spending too long on your worries and not thinking enough about your work or tasks.

* Making mistakes, forgetting things or doing less well – your brain bandwidth or "headspace" is tied up with the worry, not leaving enough for your work.
* Not entering competitions or trying out for teams or similar because you're worrying about failure.

EFFECTS ON YOUR LIFE IN GENERAL

* Lacking the courage to take exciting opportunities.
* Having low self-esteem – because you're too worried about failure.
* Having so many worries that you feel bad much of the time, instead of being able to enjoy life.
* Your friendships and relationships are affected – you might feel jealous or insecure or you might find it hard to give people what they need because you're too worried about yourself.
* Worrying about things you can't do anything about is usually a waste of time and energy.

So, although anxiety itself is meant to help you achieve and perform at your best level, sometimes it doesn't. A small number of worries shouldn't have a major immediate effect but after a while big worries can lower your enjoyment and success in life. The excellent news is that these negative effects are temporary and can be reversed when you take the steps I'm going to suggest to deal with your anxiety.

COPING WITH ANXIETY

Humans don't like anxiety – understandably! – and we typically do all sorts of things to deal with it. Some of those things are useful and positive but others are not. Some of them you can do on your own and others you'll need help with. Of course I'll show you the positive ones later, but for now I want to make you aware of the negative ones that you might come across, so that you can start to understand what the options are and why some are better than others.

NEGATIVE COPING STRATEGIES

It's important to know about these now because you might already be doing them. So you need to recognise them and understand that they are "negative" – in other words, not the best solutions!

Negative coping strategies are things that might make you feel better in the short term but which do not solve the problem and can even make it worse or create a new and different problem.

Here are some examples of negative coping strategies:

- *⋆ Biting fingernails; picking at skin; pulling hair.
- *⋆ Overeating or undereating to try to control anxiety – food is for nourishing us and enjoying.
- *⋆ Rituals that control you rather than you controlling them – such as compulsive checking.
- *⋆ Using smoking, alcohol or drugs, illegal or legal, unless prescribed by a health professional.
- *⋆ Avoiding the thing you're afraid of.

AVOIDANCE IS NOT THE ANSWER

That last one – avoidance – is probably the most common negative strategy you might be using. I'd guess everyone does it sometimes. If you're afraid of or distressed by something – school, sport, public-speaking, spiders, whatever – it's natural to want to avoid it. Avoiding it is what you want to do because that's what will feel good. But avoiding the things we fear never reduces that fear. It often makes it worse.

If your fear is affecting your life, making you stressed and spoiling your opportunities, the best thing is to reduce your anxiety response rather than avoid the thing you fear.

If you run away from a guard dog it is likely to chase you. If you learn to face it and tame it, the guard dog won't stop you living your life fully.

In Part Three you'll come across this idea often. The most important strategies are the ones that help you feel less anxious and better able to cope with worries or negative events, not ones that falsely and temporarily shield you from them. You can't stop life happening: you want to be brave and strong enough to succeed at it.

PROFESSIONAL HELP

There are times when special help can be a very good idea. When you feel that anxiety is dominating your life and spoiling your chances and success, and when you've tried some of the sensible ideas in this book and talked to the people who care about you, professional help is the next step.

If you feel that your life is being harmed by symptoms that you worry might be OCD, PTSD, phobia or another anxiety disorder, do speak to a doctor. They can tell you whether you do suffer from one of those things, or something else, or whether your anxiety is much more in the "ordinary" category of "things we just need to find ways through".

There are many things that a professional can do to help with your anxiety. It's partly that they might know more about psychology than your friends and family, and partly that talking to someone not personally connected to you can be incredibly useful. There are techniques that professional counsellors or experts use that work in ways that just talking to a sensible person might not. And sometimes the fact that the professional is not emotionally connected to you allows them to see your situation in a calmer, cooler way than someone in your family.

Part Three will tell you more about what professional help can offer. But I hope you will not need that professional help. I will show you how to stop worrying about worry and find ways to approach life with a true sense of "no worries – I can do this!" You'll learn how to train that guard dog to keep you safe and be a companion, not an enemy.

TRAINING YOUR GUARD DOG

Now we're about to come to the positive coping strategies: training your anxiety so that it becomes a useful guard dog for you, alerting you appropriately to danger, helping you become strong in the face of challenges, and sitting calmly beside you when there's no danger and you're trying to relax. First, so that you feel really up for this, let's remind ourselves of the incredible superpowers that your anxiety guard dog can bring you.

1. **It sets up your body and brain for super-performance**
    You now know that anxiety, or worry, or the stress response, consists of the chemicals adrenalin and cortisol rushing around your body. You know that the effects of this are to speed your heart and breathing so your blood vessels carry extra oxygen and power to your muscles and help you focus brilliantly on the task in hand. So, when you have a race or exam or audition or performance, you need that sense of anxiety, worry and agitation. You do not want to be super-relaxed, but super-alert.

2. **It motivates you to start preparations early enough**

   If you have exams in a few months' time and you're not at all worried about them, you probably won't get your revision started in good time. The same applies to a performance, presentation, or anything that benefits from practice, planning and careful thought. Think about training for a race: if you're too laid-back you might not start training in time or put the right amount of effort in.

3. **Worrying that something bad might happen can help you be ready if it does**

   I often advise people to focus their attention on the things that they can control, not future events that might never happen or things they can't do anything about. But that is not always my advice. There is a case for saying that occasionally it's not a bad idea to let your mind imagine the worst.

   The benefit of this is that you will have partly practised how you will cope if the very bad thing does happen. But it's crucial to make sure that you stay in control, by only allowing yourself to do it briefly and occasionally, and then letting the horrible thought go. If negative thoughts like this are big in your life, this is how anxiety can start to spoil your health and happiness. So, it's OK to worry sometimes, but not too often or for too long. And only when you choose.

4. **Worrying about something helps you focus on getting it right**

   Suppose you're part of a group organising something at school – maybe a presentation in assembly to get students to support a chosen charity. The more anxious people in the team will tend to focus on what might go wrong and take action to prevent those problems. The more laid-back people might not be thinking about these details. If I'm in a group that's organising something, I certainly want some worriers like me on the team, otherwise I'll be the only one focusing on the important details! It's our anxiety that will help make the event a huge success because we'll have acted to prevent our worries coming true. And if anything goes wrong, it won't be something we could have predicted and avoided, because, trust me, we'll have been worrying about everything possible!

When it's well-trained, your anxiety guard dog can give you all those benefits. It's really nothing to be afraid of. We just need to train it to behave well, react appropriately and sit calmly when there's nothing to worry about or nothing we can do about it.

Let the training begin!

PART THREE
STRATEGIES AND SOLUTIONS

I'm going to give you many strategies you can use to deal with your anxiety, to tame your guard dog and make it your safe companion, living peacefully outside your home and not bothering you.

When I say *many*, I really do have a lot of suggestions! So how are you going to know which to try? I've done a few things to make this easier and more effective.

Here's how this section works:

1. First, I help you analyse what type of anxiety you are dealing with right now.
2. Next I help you choose between relaxation or distraction and judge whether you want to *prevent* anxiety happening or *intervene* when it is already affecting you.
3. Then you can use the symbols to guide you to the best strategies for your particular situation.
4. Each strategy is on a separate page so you can easily record the page numbers of the ones you like and come back to them.

When you've read all the ideas, I suggest you spend time selecting the ones you like best. A great idea would be to write those down and make a card or poster for your room, so you can easily remember your favourite anxiety-reducing strategies. You'll find the strategies listed on pages 74–5 to help you with this.

LET'S WORK OUT WHAT YOU NEED

Some strategies are more suited to particular situations or problems or to different people. It's a good idea to think carefully about what is going on for you and what is right for you, rather than picking something randomly.

You also have your own abilities and disabilities and you are the best person to know whether there is something that you can't or shouldn't try. I don't want anyone to feel excluded but I am aware that I might suggest something that you simply aren't able to do or something which would be uncomfortable or wrong for you. When you see me suggest something that isn't right for you, please just move on to something else.

FIRST, KNOW YOUR ANXIETY

There are different ways of being anxious and different types of things to be anxious about. You might suffer from only one kind of anxiety or several. You might experience different worries at different times. The important thing is to be aware of how anxiety affects you, either right now or in general. Any strategies can help so do read the whole book, but I have picked a few key ones you might try first for particular situations.

TYPE OF ANXIETY	WHERE TO FIND SPECIFIC STRATEGIES
I sometimes feel nervous, panicky, tense – I actually feel like this now.	Any Instant Actions on pages 77–92: choose a breathing exercise (pages 78–85) AND a grounding exercise (pages 86–9).
I have had at least one full-on panic attack.	"Manage a panic attack" – page 92.
I have phases of anxiety – sometimes I'm fine, other times I worry about everything. I have worry chains or spirals (see page 49).	Practise some of the Instant Actions so you have one ready – pages 77–92. When you're in a worry phase, use the talking strategies on pages 179–81 and plenty of distraction actions (pages 112–23).

I get very tense/nervous about stressful things coming up – specific things, for example, a test, audition, presentation, performance, social event, school trip.	You need Instant Actions – pages 77–92.
I worry about random things that might never happen – "what if?" For example, when I hear a sad or scary news story, I worry it will happen to me or someone close to me.	See the Manage Your Mind section – pages 124–47. Try the "Build a worry box" idea on page 135.
I just have far too much to do and not enough time to do it.	Go to Manage Your Work and Time on pages 156–63.
I worry a lot about health – I'm very afraid of getting ill.	See the Manage Your Mind section – pages 124–47.
I worry a lot about things I dislike about myself or my life.	The Manage Your Mind section will help (pages 124–47), followed by any For Distraction strategies starting on page 112.
There is a particular upsetting or worrying thing in my life at the moment and it's making me very anxious.	As well as an Instant Action to use whenever you feel particularly bad (pages 77–92), you might like mindfulness strategies (pages 96–100) and talking to someone is likely to help – see Get Support on pages 179–82.
My anxieties are worse around people – I feel it's social anxiety.	You will find specific strategies for social anxiety on pages 148–53 but you will definitely also need some of the Instant Actions to lower the symptoms when they happen (pages 77–92).
I'm OK during the day but anxiety is keeping me awake at night.	See sleep advice on pages 172–75.
When I have to speak in public, I am very affected by nerves.	See "Tips for giving a talk" on pages 154–5.

SECOND, KNOW YOUR SIGNS

While you've been learning what anxiety is and how it affects people, you've also had the chance to think about how it affects you personally. Understanding and recognising your own symptoms allows you to think, "Ah, here's one of my signs of anxiety – I'd better step in with some strategies."

You have already done the quiz on page 19, but since then you've learnt so much and had time to think so it would be great to do this activity now.

On a piece of paper, draw a simple picture of a person to represent you. It could be a stick figure with your hairstyle or just a simple outline. You don't have to make it look like you, but you can if you want, as long as you represent yourself positively and kindly. It doesn't have to be artistic – but it can be if you want!

Then label it with whatever symptoms you sometimes experience when you are anxious or worried. Some examples:

Stomach-aches
Headaches
Feeling dizzy
Feeling sick
Diarrhoea
Pains in jaw
Sweating
Sleep problems
Clumsiness
Forgetfulness
Mood swings
Eczema

Your only job now is to notice when these things happen and use them as a reminder to practise your chosen strategies from this book.

NOW, PICK YOUR STRATEGIES

You'll notice in the following pages that each strategy is labelled with one or more of these symbols, which represent five categories:

Instant Actions
Emergency strategies that have a quick effect.

Prevention
Strategies that help stop you becoming anxious.

Intervention
Strategies that help once you are already feeling anxious.

Relaxation
Strategies that are properly calming.

Distraction
Strategies that distract your mind from your anxiety.

Here's a bit more to help you decide which ones to pick.

INSTANT ACTIONS

When you are feeling uncomfortably anxious, nervous or panicky, any of these strategies will have a fast effect. But you need to have practised your chosen ones first, because when you are in the middle of feeling anxious you don't want to waste time thinking about what to do.

PREVENTION OR INTERVENTION?

You can use prevention strategies to stop anxiety before it attacks. These will:

* Make you less likely to feel that anxiety is a problem.
* Make the anxiety less strong even if it does appear.
* Improve your general well-being and mental and physical health.

* Help you feel that your guard dog is sleeping peacefully outside in its kennel, not worrying you.

You can use intervention strategies when you already feel anxious. They will:

* Quickly reduce the symptoms that you are feeling now.
* Make you feel better able to deal with what you need to.
* Give you an instant tool for situations that make you feel panicky.
* Help you see that you can control your guard dog and send it back to its kennel outside.

Some strategies are great for both Prevention *and* Intervention.

RELAXATION OR DISTRACTION?

When I talk to people about anxiety and stress, I ask what relaxing activities they can think of. People of all ages come up with great ideas but usually haven't noticed that some of these ideas are not really relaxing – they are more *distracting*. Distracting activities can also be incredibly useful and healthy but sometimes you do need a relaxing activity. So, you need to know how to tell the difference and how to know when you might need a relaxation action and when you might need a distraction action.

When you choose a strategy for reducing your anxiety, there are two situations you might have. You might have both but usually you'll have one at a time.

This is where the question "relaxation or distraction?" comes in.

Relaxation situations – when you need to calm your physical symptoms. You're feeling anxious, jittery, nervous. Your heart is racing; your breathing is shallow; your stomach, face and shoulder muscles are tight. You feel the opposite of relaxed. You keep wanting to get up and move about. Perhaps you can't sleep. You might have these feelings about something in particular or you might just feel like this without knowing why.

If this is how you feel, you will benefit most from a relaxation strategy. Once you've done this and been able to reduce your symptoms, you might then also move on to a distraction strategy, but it's much better to do the relaxation first.

Distraction situations – when you need to distract your mind from a worrying or negative thought. Your mind is taking you on a worry journey and you can't stop thinking about something. Your negative or anxious thoughts are going round and round and you're imagining bad things happening. The thoughts might be keeping you awake or stopping you concentrating on important things in your day. They might be about something imaginary in the future or something that upsets you about your life or yourself.

If this is how you feel, you will benefit most from a distraction strategy. You can also add in some relaxation actions (or do them first), because they are always a good idea, but if you *only* do a relaxation action, you will find that your mind can still keep worrying. This is because relaxation actions leave plenty of attention space for the worry.

Also note that a distraction activity is more like avoiding the stress rather than dealing with it. I have talked about how avoidance is not usually the answer. However, as long as you can also deal with the symptoms by relaxing, it's really helpful to have plenty of healthy distractions up your sleeve.

As you read the strategies that follow, you will find a symbol showing which activities work well to relax you and a symbol to show which work well to distract you.

You can often work it out for yourself, too. When you think about a possible activity, ask yourself: "If I do this, how much concentration will I need? Could I, in theory, count backwards from 100 at the same time as doing this thing?"

If the answer is "Yes, I could count backwards while doing it," it's likely to be better for relaxation than distraction.

TOP TIP

It's actually best to do some of *both* types of activity during your day – relaxation and distraction. Choose different things, some which will relax, some which will distract, some which will make you laugh, some that will make you think, some social and some solo, some outdoors and some indoors, some physically active and some mentally active. Also think about which one is best for *now*, for this situation. Some strategies are neither very relaxing nor distracting but just useful strategies. And many are a mixture of both or might depend how your individual mind works. Just try to tune into how they make you feel and choose the ones that work best for you.

HOW TO FIND THE RIGHT STRATEGY

I've tried to make it easy and quick for you to find the strategy you need at any particular time. But I hope you'll read them all and make a note of the ones you like best. Here are the points to remember:

1. Each strategy is on a separate page.

2. There is a list of them on pages 74–5.

3. Each one has a combination of symbols:

   ⚡ Instant Actions

   ✚ Prevention

   ➡ Intervention

   ♥ Relaxation

   💡 Distraction

4. Choose the ones that suit you, but be open-minded and try new things – you never know what will work until you try! Ignore the ones that you are unable to do for any reason.

5. Remember to practise those strategies before you need them urgently, especially the Instant Actions on pages 77–92.

6. It's also a good idea to do the activity on page 184 once you've found the strategies that you would like to use.

THE STRATEGIES

This is a framework of the strategies to help you find what you're looking for.

THE START METHOD

Whichever other strategies you use, this is a great way to begin to respond to your anxiety. It's a neat but also comprehensive system which works beautifully with all the strategies and is easy to remember.

START stands for Stop, Take Stock, Acknowledge, Relax, Take Action. It was created by a wise psychologist friend of mine, Dr Vee Freir. You'll find her website and materials listed in the Resources. Here's what to do:

1. **Stop** – simply and firmly tell your anxious thoughts to stop and your mind to pause for a few moments. You can't deal with anxiety if your thoughts carry on spinning out of control. (You'll find suggestions for how to stop your thoughts on page 131.)

2. **Take stock** – now that you've stopped your thoughts spinning, you can focus on the true situation, rather than your imagined, panicky one. What is actually happening? What is really going on in your body and around you? Is the situation exactly as you thought or is this just how your mind and body are reacting?

3. **Acknowledge** – next, just acknowledge that you are feeling whatever you are feeling. Accept your feelings as being natural, real and temporary. "I feel like this right now." They will not harm you – they are there to alert you to a possible situation.

4. **Relax** – now you can use one of the Instant Actions from pages 77–92. This will lower your anxiety so your body and mind are able to take the next step.

5. **Take action** – once you have some control of your body's reaction, you can do things to improve your situation. For example, you might break down the challenge into small steps and start tackling them. Or you might make a timetable or list. Or you might ask for help.

INSTANT ACTIONS

On the next pages, you'll find lots of fast-acting strategies to deal with anxious feelings. These are powerful ways to help you feel calmer. Use them when you have symptoms such as a fast heart rate, shallow breathing, tight muscles or any feelings of discomfort in your body and worry in your mind.

What to do with these ideas:

1. Try several breathing strategies and grounding strategies until you find one of each that you like best.

2. Practise them before you need them. When anxiety strikes, you want to use your strategy without delay. And the more you've practised, the more automatic it will be.

3. Also practise the "Do the opposite" strategy on page 90 – it's a really useful idea.

4. If you suffer panic attacks, practise the "Manage a panic attack" strategy on page 92, too.

It doesn't matter whether you are anxious about something specific or not: these tips will calm you quickly.

We all need these relaxation skills so do teach your friends and adults!

BREATHING STRATEGIES

These are really essential techniques that every human needs. They instantly dial down the responses in your body when you are hit by anxiety. They work for mild and severe anxiety.

There are different ways of focusing on and controlling your breath. All have the same effects, but different people find some work for them better than others. Try them all and then choose the one you like best. Practise until you've got the hang of it. That's now your personal breath tool.

BREATHING STRATEGY 1 | BELLY BREATHING

When you're stressed, you usually breathe with your upper chest, so your breath is quite shallow. Notice how it feels when you consciously soften your stomach area and allow it to move as you breathe. It's a deeper, less tense breathing. You're more relaxed. Welcome to belly breathing!

WHAT TO DO

1. Lie comfortably on the floor or a bed. (You can also do this in a chair, but to start with it's often easier lying down or at least lying back in a relaxing chair.)

2. Place one hand on your belly, just below your ribs, and one hand on your upper chest.

3. Take a slow, deep breath in through your nose and feel your belly go outwards.

4. As you breathe out, feel your belly go in. (Don't push it in; it will naturally go in and relax.)

5. Do this around eight to ten times, noticing the movement of your belly out and in.

When you've got the hang of this, do the same in a sitting position and then in a standing position. After a while, you won't need to put your hands on your belly and chest as you'll be able to feel the correct movements without them. Your hands are just there to help focus your mind in the right place.

TIP
There's a good YouTube video of belly breathing in the Resources. Or just do an online search for "belly breathing + video".

| **BREATHING STRATEGY 2** | **4-7-8 BREATHING** |

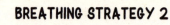

This encourages you to use counting as a breathing focus, rather than the movement of your belly. But you should still think about your belly moving out as you breathe in, as this will help the relaxation effect.

BEFORE YOU START

★ You might find that these particular numbers don't work well for you. Personally I find that 7 and 8 are both a little too long, so I do 4-5-7. The important things are: a) the breathing out should be longer than the breathing in; and b) counting is important as it helps keep you thinking about your breath.

★ The counting should be around the speed of seconds; to make this easier you can say "one alligator, two alligator".

★ If you become dizzy or light-headed, stop. Try using a different choice of numbers.

WHAT TO DO

1. Lie or sit comfortably.

2. Breathe in through your nose as you count to four (or whatever works for you). If you can't breathe easily through your nose, it doesn't matter.

3. Hold your breath as you count to seven.

4. Breathe out through your mouth as you count to eight.

5. Do this four times – don't do more than this at first. You can build up to ten once you can do it without feeling dizzy.

BREATHING STRATEGY 3	SQUARE BREATHING

Another way to focus on your breath to calm yourself down is square breathing.

WHAT TO DO

1. Sit or lie comfortably.
2. Imagine a square shape in front of you. Focus on the bottom left corner.
3. Breathing in through your nose, visualise your breath going up the left-hand side to the next corner.
4. Holding your breath, visualise moving across the top of the square to the top right corner.
5. Breathing out through your mouth, visualise your breath sliding down the right-hand side.
6. Holding your breath, visualise moving along the bottom of the square to the starting point.
7. Do this five to ten times.

TIP
Triangle breathing is the same principle but you breathe in for one side of the triangle, hold for the second side and breathe out for the third side.

| BREATHING STRATEGY 4 | FIVE-FINGER BREATHING |

This is helpful for people who find it hard to visualise images.

WHAT TO DO

1. Sitting upright and comfortably, hold your left hand in front of you with the palm facing away. Your thumb will be to the right.

2. Take the pointing finger of your right hand and place it at the base of your left thumb, where it meets your wrist.

3. As you breathe in, move that finger to the top of your left thumb. Hold it there and hold your breath for a couple of seconds.

4. As you breathe out, move the finger down the other side of the thumb. Hold it there for a couple of seconds.

5. As you breathe in again, move the finger to the top of the first finger and as you breathe out, move it down the other side of that finger, each time holding your breath for a couple of seconds as you reach the top and bottom of a finger.

6. Continue for each finger and then go back again until you reach your starting point.

BREATHING STRATEGY 5 | BREATHING WITH GIFS

There are lots of gifs online that help you focus your breath. They can be very helpful for people who find it hard to visualise.

You will find examples by doing an internet search for "breathing gifs" or "gifs to help me relax". It's a matter of personal choice which you pick. You don't need to pay and do avoid any which come with advertisements, as they will be distracting and unrelaxing.

You need quick access to one and not to scroll through websites trying to find one, as that is not relaxing and you might find yourself waylaid by something exciting! So, once you've found one you like, save it to your device and go straight to it when needed.

Once you've used it a few times, you might find you can visualise it without using your device. This would be perfect.

WHAT TO DO

1. Often there are instructions with the gif, or it might be obvious how to use it. Breathe in and out, slowly, in time to the movement of the gif.

2. Focusing your eyes on the gif and your mind on your breathwork takes just the right amount of concentration, and you will find yourself feeling calmer.

BREATHING STRATEGY 6 | HOT CHOCOLATE BREATHING

This is a neat exercise that combines meditation with breath control. It uses guided visualisation and combines all the senses, while also giving your hands something to do. Teachers often use it in classrooms as it's something that almost all students can relate to.

WHAT TO DO

1. Sit comfortably. You can have eyes closed or open.

2. Put your hands in front of you as though holding a delicious hot drink. (Though not too hot to hold comfortably!)

3. Think about the feeling of warmth in your hands and the shape and feel of the mug.

4. Bring the "mug" close to your face and, breathing in through your nose, imagine the smell of the drink.

5. Breathe out firmly but smoothly through your mouth, imagining that you are cooling the drink.

6. Breathe in and out like this several times. When you think the "drink" is cool enough, take an imaginary sip and think about the taste and feeling as it goes down your throat.

TIP

If you don't like the thought of hot chocolate, you can choose any hot drink!

BREATHING STRATEGY 7 | BREATHE IT OUT

How often have you heard people say "take a deep breath" or "take three deep breaths"? There's a problem with this: when you're tense, you're already breathing shallowly, at the top of your chest, and if you immediately breathe in (taking a breath) you're going to be doing it even more. Much better is to breathe out first – to let it out, not in.

WHAT TO DO

1. **When you catch yourself feeling anxious and breathing shallowly and high in your chest, expel the air like a sigh.**

2. **When you breathe in again, take little notice of that in-breath, but focus more on pushing it out, hard, through your mouth.**

3. **As you push it out, visualise the tension going with it. Let your shoulders fall and your stomach soften.**

4. **Continue for three to four breaths, each time taking a slow breath in (ideally though your nose) but pushing it out hard with a whooshing noise.**

> **TIP**
> If you've chosen this as your go-to breathing technique, I recommend you also practise one of the earlier ones, as this one is so quick that it might not be enough.

GROUNDING OR CENTRING STRATEGIES

These two words mean the same. I prefer "grounding". When you are very anxious, your thoughts can be all over the place. They could be flitting about in the past (worrying about things that have happened), the present (panicking about what's happening now) or the future (stressing about things that might never happen or at least aren't happening now).

There are three main situations when grounding can be an important instant strategy:

1. When you have something you want or need to focus on right now – such as a task, deadline, urgent action – and your spiralling thoughts are preventing you.

2. When your spinning thoughts are dominating your mind and preventing you focusing on positive or useful things or enjoying your life.

3. When you start to feel panicky in a particular situation that distresses you, such as a crowded train or a very noisy place.

In these situations, you need something to focus on that will keep you here and now – "grounded" – so that you can regain your control and do what you need or want to do.

It's a bit like having someone gently tap you on the shoulder and say, "Come on – you're OK. Just focus on this."

Some ideas are on the next three pages. Choose the ones you like.

GROUNDING STRATEGY 1 | 5-4-3-2-1

This is a simple and very effective grounding technique to help your anxious mind.

BEFORE YOU START

✱ You're going to be asked to notice objects. If you are dealing with unpleasant things near you, try to choose objects not directly connected with your stress. For example, if you are entering an exam, notice neutral things such as the sky, trees, the sound of a distant voice, not things like another anxious student or a big sign about the exam.

✱ If you have a sensory impairment, use imagination instead. For example, when I was writing this I had lost my smell and taste through Covid, but I could remember smells and tastes so I could still do the activity in my mind.

WHAT TO DO

1. Notice five things you can see.
2. Four things you can touch.
3. Three things you can hear – if you listen hard enough you might hear wind, buzzing electricity, a bird, distant voices, the sound of your breath.
4. Two things you can smell.
5. And one you can taste.
6. That's all! The simple mental act of noticing things around you will ground you.

> **TIP**
> You could now do one of the breathing strategies from the previous pages.

GROUNDING STRATEGY 2 | 3-3-3

Here's a quicker version of the first strategy which could be even better when panic is welling up.

WHAT TO DO

1. **Notice and focus on three things you can touch; think about the differences.**

2. **Do the same with three things you can hear.**

3. **And move three parts of your body in different ways.**

Why three? It's a nice number! There's not really any magic to it. Do four or five if you prefer!

· ·

TIP

You can adapt this in lots of ways. You could create a routine of three movements or stretches and do them three times. You could clench your fists and relax them three times. You could pick up three books or pens or other objects and judge which is heavier. Anything which involves noticing something physical in your surroundings and connecting yourself to it will help you with grounding yourself.

GROUNDING STRATEGY 3 | GROUNDING WITH A SENSE

Sometimes you forget that you're connected to the physical world around you. Often all you need is something extremely simple to remind you that you are here, now, not floating in space.

WHAT TO DO

1. Choose touch, smell or taste and find an object that will use that sense.

   - *⁖* Touch: perhaps an ice cube, a mug of hot water or a prickly brush.
   - *⁖* Smell: perhaps a flower, bar of soap, strong-smelling food.
   - *⁖* Taste: anything you love the taste of. Keep it on your tongue rather than chewing or swallowing it immediately.

2. Spend a minute focusing on the thing you've chosen, noticing your breathing as you do.

3. That's all! You can do it again with something else if you want.

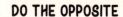

DO THE OPPOSITE

You know that your body reacts in certain ways to stress or anxiety and that not everyone reacts the same. "Doing the opposite" involves noticing what your body is doing in reaction to anxiety or stress and making it do the opposite. It allows you to take control of your body, just like taking the lead of your dog and correcting the behaviour.

Think of it like this: your body did the right thing in reacting – just as your guard dog does the right thing by barking when it detects danger. But the guard dog does not need to keep barking once the owner has got the message. In fact, when dogs keep barking it's annoying and stressful!

On the next page, you'll find examples of how you might put this into practice to reduce your anxiety quickly.

OPPOSITE IDEAS

When you notice anything your body or mind is doing in reaction to stress, try deliberately doing the opposite and notice that it makes you feel more relaxed. As you become more aware of your body's reaction to anxiety, this will become easier. Here are some examples.

THINGS TO TRY

* If your breathing is fast, slow it down.

* If you are breathing *in* too much, breathe *out* more.

* If you're breathing high up in your chest, bring your breathing action down to your belly. (Remember belly breathing from page 79.)

* If your stomach feels tense, relax it.

* If you are clenching your teeth or jaw, consciously soften the muscles there. (Tip: hold the tip of your tongue to the roof of your mouth, just behind your front teeth.)

* If your mind is telling you to run away (but there is no actual danger that you should run from), concentrate on staying where you are but focusing on your chosen breathing and grounding strategies.

* If you crave food that you know is a poor choice, enjoy a few mouthfuls of delicious fruit or crunchy nuts.

* If you start to bite your fingers or pick at skin, give yourself something different to do with your fingers.

Be proud of what you just did: you gave your guard dog a useful training session.

MANAGE A PANIC ATTACK

Before you read on, make sure you have practised one of the breathing techniques. Perhaps also look back at page 47 where I describe panic attacks.

WHAT TO DO

1. Remind yourself – aloud or in your head – that a panic attack cannot harm you. It is only your body producing too much adrenalin and it will stop soon.

2. Focus on your body. Place the tip of your tongue on the roof of your mouth, just behind your teeth. Gently keep it there. (It helps you to relax your jaw and face.)

3. Begin your chosen breathing technique.

4. Feel your breathing soften and relax and your heart rate settle.

5. Start to notice ordinary things: how you can smell your skin, hear the sounds around you, feel the sensation of touching objects. Everything is fine, normal.

6. Try your chosen grounding technique.

TIP

Show this to family and friends, so they know how to help when you have an attack. They can repeat that nothing bad will happen and help you focus on your breath. Once you start to feel calmer, they can help by distracting you, perhaps making you laugh. But in the middle of your attack, distraction will not help as your feelings will be too strong. (And distraction at that moment is avoidance, which we don't want.) They need to stay with you and repeat calming words and actions. Although panic attacks are harmless, they stop you enjoying life or having the success you deserve. If they are a big problem, seek professional help.

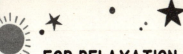

FOR RELAXATION

On page 70 you learnt about the difference between situations where you might need relaxation and others where you might need distraction. The Instant Actions which you've already met are obviously relaxing but there are lots more things you can choose from.

The next few pages offer enjoyable relaxation activities. They will generally help your body slow its heart rate and breathing and reduce the responses associated with anxiety, such as sweating, nausea and feeling jittery and tense. You might do any of them after you've done one of the Instant Actions.

You can do these things when you're actually feeling anxious (as interventions) but they are also brilliant as preventions. Pick several that suit you and do one or two every day, whenever you have a chance. Why not write one in your diary for every day?

The more anxious you feel, the more important it is to build a variety of such activities into your day. Don't wait for weekends or holidays: relaxation is part of healthy life, not a luxury!

PREVENT A DELAYED REACTION

On page 32 I talked about how you might have a delayed reaction if you bottle up your feelings of anxiety during a traumatic experience. A delayed reaction is when you have an upsetting response a while after the event is over – like a guard dog barking after the danger has gone.

If you are going through an extremely frightening or distressing event right now, I have some suggestions to help manage your response now and reduce the risk of a delayed reaction later.

WHAT TO DO

1. If you feel very anxious or distressed, it's OK to say so. It's OK to find it hard to sleep, for your appetite to change and to struggle to make good decisions or concentrate on ordinary things. It is not a weakness. Don't try to ignore or dismiss these normal reactions. Of course, you want to stay in control in order to take necessary action, but don't try too hard to keep feelings hidden for long.

2. Find someone to share your worries with. If your close family is too preoccupied or upset you might want to choose someone else. You need someone who will listen and accept how you're feeling.

3. If you can't find the right person, contact Childline (in the UK) or any helpline for young people – see the Resources.

4. If you can do any of your normal activities such as exercise or seeing your friends, do that. You might not feel like it but it will help you.

MANAGE A DELAYED REACTION

If you have gone through something traumatic and felt that you held yourself together at the time but now feel very emotional or vulnerable, page 32 might reassure you, as I went through this recently (not for the first time).

I have some suggestions for you if this is happening now or if it happens again.

WHAT TO DO

1. Say to yourself, "This is just a delayed reaction: there's nothing wrong with me. My body and brain are only telling me to pause and look after myself."

2. Use the breathing and grounding techniques that you've learnt.

3. From the previous page, follow the advice about talking to someone.

4. Accept that you need a bit of time – it might be hours or it might be longer – to get your mental strength and balance back. This will partly happen through the healing nature of time, but also through you bringing positive experiences and thoughts into your life – see the next point.

5. Think about which activities in your life give you pleasure and do whichever you can: perhaps see a close friend, go for an ice cream with friends, watch a favourite film, bake a cake, make a video, have a bath, give yourself a hand massage (page 110) or go for a walk.

MINDFULNESS

Mindfulness is a well-known approach which lots of people find very helpful for managing anxiety. You can do a course, either in person or online, or you can teach yourself, following instructions on a suitable website or in a book. You might find classes at your local library.

The next pages offer ways of bringing mindfulness into your life, but first there are a few things to know.

WHAT YOU NEED TO KNOW

★ **Mindfulness might be relaxing or distracting for you, or a mixture. It depends what goes on in your mind while you are doing it. It is more likely to be relaxing, however, so I have used the symbol for relaxation.**

★ **If a negative thought appears while you're practising mindfulness, just acknowledge it and let it go. Focus back on what you're meant to be thinking about.**

★ **Mindfulness is not good for everyone. Because it asks you to focus on things in and around you *now*, you might find yourself focusing on things that make you uncomfortable; it might even make your mental state worse. If you have been diagnosed with a mental health disorder, check with your medical practitioner whether they recommend mindfulness for you. This is especially true if you have been diagnosed with Post-Traumatic Stress Disorder.**

★ **If mindfulness makes you feel worse or doesn't work for you, don't do it.**

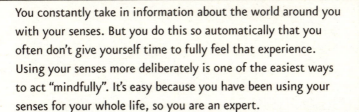

You constantly take in information about the world around you with your senses. But you do this so automatically that you often don't give yourself time to fully feel that experience. Using your senses more deliberately is one of the easiest ways to act "mindfully". It's easy because you have been using your senses for your whole life, so you are an expert.

WHAT TO DO

1. Choose a time when you won't be interrupted and when you can give at least ten minutes, and ideally more, to this activity.

2. Make yourself comfortable. You can be in any position you like as long as you're not uncomfortable or unsafe.

3. Go through each sense in turn, spending a couple of minutes using it to detect everything possible in your environment. With each one, you'll start by noticing the most obvious things, but then you'll spot small things you hadn't noticed before – a tiny crack in a wall, a humming sound, the fact that what you thought was a smooth table actually has minuscule ridges. It doesn't matter what you notice – the point is the focusing.

TIP

If you lack any particular sense, just focus on the others. But if one sense has a partial impairment, as long as it's not painful or you've been told not to, you can still focus on it and do your best. It won't make mindfulness any harder.

MINDFUL STRATEGY 2	DAILY ACTIVITIES

This strategy is going to sound incredibly simple but it's surprisingly difficult to do for more than a few seconds. The fact that it's difficult is one of the things that makes it effective for anxiety: it can help you take your mind off the thing you're anxious about. This means it can be distracting as well as relaxing, especially when you're doing it well.

WHAT TO DO

1. **Pick any simple, familiar activity that does not involve talking to someone or concentrating. It could be showering, getting dressed, doing hair and make-up, shaving, making your breakfast or a snack, walking to school or the shops, putting your things in your locker, a bus journey, being the passenger in a car or getting ready for bed.**

2. **Focus on the details of the activity while you're doing it. Keep all your attention on these actions. If you find other thoughts coming in, gently pull your focus back to the task.**

3. **Start to be aware of everything you don't normally notice: what your hands are doing, the order you do it in, your surroundings, how you feel, your breath and heart rate. Think about your joints, muscles and skin.**

4. **Do this two or three times a day for a few minutes or however long the activity takes. Do it whenever you think of it. Each time, notice yourself feeling calmer.**

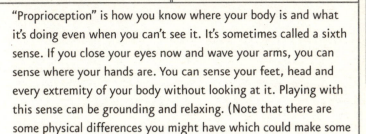

MINDFUL STRATEGY 3 | YOUR BODY IN SPACE

"Proprioception" is how you know where your body is and what it's doing even when you can't see it. It's sometimes called a sixth sense. If you close your eyes now and wave your arms, you can sense where your hands are. You can sense your feet, head and every extremity of your body without looking at it. Playing with this sense can be grounding and relaxing. (Note that there are some physical differences you might have which could make some of this exercise difficult or impossible. Just do what you can.)

WHAT TO DO

1. Sit down and close your eyes. Keep your eyes closed for the whole exercise. Mentally scan your body as it remains still, thinking about your feet and your hands without moving them.

2. Now hold your hands out in front of you. Wiggle your fingers and rotate your wrists. Think about and sense them.

3. Make the pointing fingers of each hand touch each other. (You might be very slightly out but you'll basically be able to do this with your eyes shut, unless you are very tired or you have a problem with proprioception. Some medications make this harder, too.)

4. Touch one finger to your nose. Touch your hands together behind your back. Touch each ear with each hand in turn.

5. Stretch each foot out and slowly rotate the ankle. Bend and straighten each leg a few times at the knee if you can. Now touch each knee with each hand.

6. If you kept your eyes shut, you proved your proprioception skills and practised them at the same time. You should also feel more relaxed and more grounded.

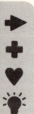

MINDFUL STRATEGY 4	FOCUS ON ONE THING

A simple strategy is to choose one sense and an object relating to it and notice things about that object. Because you have to focus, it might be distracting as well as relaxing.

WHAT TO DO

1. **Choose one of these suggestions or think of your own:**

   * **Hold an ice cube. Feel the cold, wet slipperiness. Notice how you want to wipe up the water – resist this and slow your breathing. Hold it until it is liquid.**

   * **Put an ice cube in your mouth. Notice the hard slipperiness, the cool water sliding down your throat. Visualise the water making its way through your body.**

   * **Find something prickly – hairbrush, scourer, rough doormat – and press it gently on your skin. How does it feel on your palm compared with on your cheek?**

   * **Put a slice of three different fruits in identical dishes. Put them in front of you on a table, close your eyes and move them so you don't know which is which. With eyes still shut, pick up one bowl and use smell to identify the fruit. Describe it in words. Do the same with the others. Then put one in your mouth and do the same with taste and the texture. Can you describe this? Do the same with all the pieces of fruit.**

2. **Do this for several minutes a day and notice how you feel calmer and how it gets easier. If negative thoughts come, notice them and watch them wander away.**

MEDITATION

Mindfulness and meditation are similar but not the same. Mindfulness asks you to notice particular aspects of the world around you in an alert but relaxed way. It does not try to stop worries coming in, but helps you live with those worries without being threatened by them. This makes mindfulness very good as a relaxation strategy (for many people) but usually less good as a distraction strategy.

In meditation, you focus your mind on something specific, so that you move away from and forget whatever your worries are. The concentration is more intense than in mindfulness – in mindfulness you notice things around you; in meditation you focus harder on a target object, either in your mind or an actual object in front of you. This makes meditation a useful distraction strategy, as well as being relaxing.

On the next pages are a couple of ways you can practise simple strategies that are more like meditation than mindfulness.

On the internet, you can also look for "guided meditations", where you listen to a recorded voice helping direct your mind. Search "free guided meditations" and make sure you choose one that is appropriate for your age.

MEDITATION STRATEGY 1 | BODY SCAN

This uses your own body as the focus for your mind. It can be deeply relaxing for many people. Sometimes it can be sufficiently mind-occupying to be a distraction, too.

WHAT TO DO

1. **Make yourself comfortable. Ensure that you will not be disturbed.**

2. **You can have gentle music playing, if you wish. Try whale music or white noise like waves or running water. You'll find some online.**

3. **Close your eyes for the best effect. If you'd rather not, that's fine.**

4. **Relax, slow and soften your breathing.**

5. **Focus on your toes and feet. You can wriggle your toes or rotate your ankles a few times if you want. Then relax them. Relax them more. Do this for a few breaths.**

6. **Move your focus to calves and knees. Again, relax them, feeling them soften more deeply with each breath.**

7. **Slowly move your focus up your body, stopping for a few breaths at each group of muscles. You'll go through your buttocks, stomach, chest, shoulders, down your arms to your hands. Then to neck, jaw, up the back of your head; down your face, eyes, cheeks and mouth. Spend more time on all the muscles in your face, as this usually holds a lot of tension.**

8. **Either start again or focus on any part of your body, feeling it in your mind, being aware how you're sinking into a deeper and softer relaxation.**

MEDITATION STRATEGY 2 | VISUALISE YOUR HAPPY

You can significantly lower your heart rate by thinking about and imagining yourself in a place where you feel very relaxed. Anyone can do this but if you practise often you'll find two advantages: first, you'll instantly be able to decide what you're going to visualise so you won't waste time wondering; and second, you'll get better at it. This is a very simple way into meditation.

WHAT TO DO

1. Make yourself comfortable and try to ensure you won't be disturbed for a few minutes.

2. Close your eyes.

3. Do your chosen breathing strategy for a few breaths.

4. Imagine yourself in a place where you feel happy. It could be an actual place or somewhere in your imagination.

5. Build the details – the more detail, the stronger your meditation will be and the more you will enjoy it. You might start with what you can see but don't ignore any of the senses: what can you hear, smell, taste and feel on your skin? Is it warm or cold? Can you feel the breeze? What do you love about this place? What are you thinking when you're there?

6. Stay in your happy place for as long as you're able.

TIP

On the next page you'll find more guidance for visualising yourself in a happy place.

On the previous page, I asked you to imagine yourself in a place where you feel happy. But some people find that difficult, so here are two guided visualisations for you. Choose the one you prefer.

WHAT TO DO

1. **Get comfortable, ideally where you won't be disturbed for a while. Close your eyes and spend a minute focusing on your breath, letting it slow, deepen, relax.**

2. **Take your mind to any beautiful place you can imagine. Here are two ideas:**

   ✱ **You're lying in a hammock, in a beautiful garden edged by rustling trees. It's a sunny day, and you're in dappled shade, a perfect temperature. You have no pressures, no tasks; the holiday stretches ahead. No one is going to disturb you. You're safe. Within reach, there's a delicious iced drink of watermelon, mango and fresh lime. The scent of roses passes on the breeze. Your muscles sink into deep relaxation as your mind slows and wanders.**

   ✱ **You're walking at the edge of a calm sea. The sand is wrinkled beneath your bare feet. Your worries are washed away on the salt breeze. You feel the morning sun on your skin, the water around your feet as the tiny waves come in, and out, and in, and out. You start to run and you hold your arms out to the side, letting the air try to push you. You are flying across the rippling sand and your energy is growing. Soon you slow to a walk again and focus on the feeling of the water and air and sunlight. You smile and your heart lifts. Life is good.**

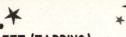

EFT (TAPPING)

EFT – sometimes called "tapping" – stands for Emotional Freedom Technique and it's used for anxiety, pain and Post-Traumatic Stress Disorder (PTSD). It is not proven but may work on the same principles as acupressure and acupuncture, which are both well supported by research.

EFT – along with acupuncture and acupressure – is based on the theory that our bodies have channels of energy, and that we can help emotional and physical pain by unblocking those channels when we apply pressure to certain points in the body, called meridians.

EFT is something you can teach yourself, although only an expert could make sure you were doing it correctly. You'll find more detailed instructions via the links in the Resources, but here is my basic interpretation so you get the idea.

The tapping points are in the following places:

1. **The "karate chop" point – the side of your hand, as if you were doing a karate chop.**
2. **Top of your head.**
3. **Above your eye – edge of your eyebrow towards your nose.**
4. **Side of your eye – on the bony part.**
5. **Under your eye – again, on the bone.**
6. **Under your nose.**
7. **Under your lip – in the crease or dimple.**
8. **Under your collarbone – 2.5 cm under, in the middle.**
9. **Under your armpit – a hand-width below.**

See the next page for how to do it!

HOW TO DO EFT TAPPING

BEFORE YOU START

★ Most of the tapping points occur on both sides of the body but you don't have to do both sides and you don't have to tap the same side for all.

★ You can use whichever hand you want.

★ Using more than one finger makes sure you hit the right spot.

★ Your "set-up statement" needs to focus on a problem of yours, not someone else's. If your anxiety is about someone else, find something you want to change within you. For example, if you are anxious about whether people like you, it's your anxiety about this that is the issue, not what other people think.

WHAT TO DO

1. Identify the tapping points. (See previous page.)

2. Decide the problem you want to address and create an "accepting" statement about it. This is called the "set-up". For example, "Although I worry about ..., I deeply and completely accept myself."

3. Repeat the statement while tapping the first point (the karate point) several times with two or three fingers, until you feel confident.

4. Tap each point, in order, around five times.

5. Notice whether your negative feeling or anxiety reduces during this.

OTHER RELAXING ACTIVITIES

The ideas below can all work for relaxation. Remember: if you have to concentrate hard, it's likely to be good for distraction from worries but might not be genuinely relaxing. Notice whether each one is relaxing or distracting when you do it.

WHAT TO DO

1. Pick any of the following and do one every day.

   ✳ Have a bath – set aside time and make the room welcoming and just how you like it; use bath products that you love; turn your phone off and leave it outside the room.

   ✳ Listen to music – not as background to another task. Music can affect mood so choose some that will do what you want: raise your spirits or calm you – it's your choice.

   ✳ Give yourself a manicure, pedicure or facial – you and a friend could do this for each other.

   ✳ Colour in – you'll find lots online to download and colour.

   ✳ Doodle – get inspiration online if you need. (But don't get drawn into infinite scrolling!)

2. As you do your chosen activity, remind yourself that this is to improve mental health and deal with anxiety. These things are not luxuries but important for health.

TIP
See the next page for one of the best genuinely relaxing things you can do.

TUNE INTO NATURE

A lot of research points to nature benefiting people's mental state. When you can look at or be part of a natural scene – anything with greenery or seascape – your heart rate slows, stress reduces and mood lifts. There's even research suggesting that people heal from illness or injury faster when they have a natural view.

But what if you live in a city? Let me show you some options.

WHAT TO DO

1. Find an image online and load it as your screensaver. Or find several images and create a folder you can look at any time. You can choose woods, rolling hillsides, the sea, fields of sheep. Or find highly magnified images of a flower or an insect and marvel at the intricacy of nature.

2. Listen to the sounds of nature. If you search "natural soundscapes" online you'll find loads – including free on Spotify, for example. Use it as a background while you do meditation or your breathwork practice.

3. If you listen to those sounds while also looking at natural landscapes, even better. For example, you might sit in a park while listening to a recording of birdsong.

4. Is there somewhere you could visit at the weekend? Keep your phone in your pocket and just enjoy being in greenery or at the seaside.

5. Go to a local park with trees and grass. Spend time properly looking at plants, put your hands on the bark of a tree, sit on a bench and listen to birdsong, or lie on the grass to watch the clouds.

FACIAL SELF-MASSAGE

This costs nothing! Pressing various points in your face releases tension and just taking time to do something relaxing like this has benefits. It can also be a mindful activity.

WHAT TO DO

1. Set up a peaceful, comfortable place, ideally in your bedroom or bathroom. Make it as relaxing as possible, considering lighting, temperature and scent.

2. Get into comfortable clothes. Remove shoes, jewellery and glasses. Wash and dry your hands.

3. If you want, use cream or oil that is appropriate for your face. You can even use olive oil. (If you have oily skin or you're prone to spots, choose something non-oily.) If you don't want to use anything, that's fine!

4. Sitting comfortably, take a few slow breaths to relax and loosen stomach muscles.

5. With two fingers of each hand, slowly massage your temples in small circles.

6. Gradually move your circling fingers around your temples, then to your eyes – above, to the side and then along the bone beneath. Then down the side of your cheeks, beside your ear; round your jawbone to the centre of your jaw, up your chin, round the outside edges of your mouth and up your cheeks beside your nose until you reach your eyes again and back to your temples.

7. Any areas that feel particularly good, spend extra time there. Feel yourself relax, your breath soften, your shoulders sink.

HAND OR FOOT SELF-MASSAGE

I'm sure that having a hand or foot massage from an expert therapist takes this to a different level, but doing it for yourself is easy, relaxing and free (apart from a bit of cream or oil). And your hands and feet will feel and look great afterwards.

WHAT TO DO

1. Prepare as for a facial massage (see the previous page).

2. Ideally, you need hand or body cream or oil, but there's no need for anything expensive and it doesn't matter whether it's for hands, feet or body – it's all your skin! Again, olive oil or other edible oil will be fine.

3. Wash and dry hands. Do the same for your feet if you're massaging them.

4. Apply the cream or oil to your hands and massage every area of each hand and foot. Use your thumbs to press into any muscle tension. There should be no pain – if there is, stop massaging that bit – but the pressure should feel firm.

5. Here are some extra hints:

    ✱ Try to follow a pattern rather than going randomly from place to place – for example, each finger in turn, each toe in turn, keep massaging in one direction, and try to do the second hand or foot in a similar way to the first.

    ✱ Gently pull or stretch the fingers and toes.

    ✱ Don't forget the very tips of fingers and toes.

    ✱ Keep the hand or foot that's being massaged as relaxed as you can.

    ✱ Imagine your tension being massaged away.

USE A WEIGHTED BLANKET

If you haven't heard of weighted blankets, they might seem an odd idea. But there's convincing research that they work and many people find them helpful. They were originally used to help people with autism, because the main role of these blankets is to soothe and comfort and autistic people often deal with extreme anxiety.

Weighted blankets can help with anxiety, sleep problems and even depression. The reason they work may be that the weight of the blanket around you is like being hugged.

Unfortunately, weighted blankets are not cheap, although the price has come down as they've become more popular. Perhaps some relatives could club together for your birthday?

WHAT TO DO

1. You need to choose a blanket that is right for your own size and weight. Any company selling the blankets should offer clear information on that. They should also allow a window for return if it's not right for you.

2. Use your blanket for fifteen minutes at first. Do it while you relax on a sofa, chair or bed. You can wrap it round specific parts of your body, such as legs or shoulders – it's up to you.

3. You can also use it at the end of a yoga session to aid relaxation, or during a mindfulness or meditation session.

4. Feel the comforting weight helping your muscles relax, your heart rate and breathing slow. Take time to notice how it makes you feel.

FOR DISTRACTION

You've now got lots of relaxation strategies but you know these might not work so well for managing worrying thoughts. When you have intrusive negative thoughts buzzing round your mind, you need strategies that occupy a large amount of concentration so that there's no room for the negative thoughts.

From the suggestions on the next pages, choose any you like the sound of. Everyone's different and some things won't work for you, but others will. I do encourage you to try new things sometimes, though!

You might also get a sense of relaxation after doing these activities, but I have used the distraction symbol because that is the specific purpose. Another value is that they are healthy activities to use as breaks in your work, too.

You might think that a distraction strategy could be a form of avoidance. This is partly why I've given you the relaxation suggestions first – because they are absolutely essential and need to be used first. But distractions are also very healthy, especially when used after a genuine relaxation strategy. And you can't spend all your time actively relaxing! A balance of relaxation and distraction, along with your work, sleeping, eating and other aspects of life, is the aim.

BE SOCIAL

Being with other people can be a distraction from worries and being alone can make us overthink. So, spending time with friends or making new friends is a good way to reduce worry time and can also lead to new opportunities and even skills.

Not everyone enjoys being with lots of other people and it's perfectly natural to find social activity unrelaxing, even stressful. My advice is: try to work out which type of interaction with people you do like or can do, and find opportunities for that. You don't have to be in a big group – being with one or two people is equally effective.

If you're naturally quiet, you might need to push yourself sometimes. If you're socially anxious, you might need more help. There is a whole section starting on page 148 that will help you with social anxiety and speaking in front of other people.

WHAT TO DO

1. **Arrange to meet one or more friends at the cinema, coffee shop, someone's house.**
2. **Find an after-school activity, such as drama or a craft workshop.**
3. **Plan a meal with friends where you each bring a dish.**
4. **Find people with a shared interest and spend time exploring and enjoying it with them.**
5. **Plan a trip or picnic or walk.**
6. **Be social online. Be sure to chat to similar-aged people and let an adult know if you are talking to people you haven't met. Never meet someone for the first time alone.**

TIP
If you feel too anxious to try those ideas, look at page 149.

EXPRESS YOURSELF IN WRITING

If this isn't something you've tried before, it might be difficult at first. But writing your thoughts down or using any way to express yourself in written words is a good way to deal with anxiety. It can be very satisfying, too.

There are three ways to approach this:

1. **Write down your own worries.**

2. **Write a journal – the good and bad things that happen to you or just random thoughts from your day.**

3. **Just write – make things up and be creative!**

On the next three pages, I'll tackle each of those in turn. Whichever you try, you have some other choices:

★ You can use paper and pen or a computer or other device.

★ You don't have to show anyone what you've written. If you don't want someone else to read it, use a made-up name and take any other steps to keep it secret.

★ You don't have to worry about spelling or punctuation or handwriting. This is just for you.

> **TIP**
> It's very important to switch off your phone and any internet-enabled device to help you focus on writing.

| **WRITING STRATEGY 1** | **WRITE DOWN YOUR WORRIES** |

There are two particular times when this can be useful. First, when you're going through or have just gone through a bad experience and you want to deal with it and feel better. And, second, when you're trying to go to sleep and you want to stop the repeated anxious thoughts.

WHAT TO DO

1. If you're trying to describe something bad that's happening or has happened, write in the third person ("he", "she" or "they" instead of "I"). This helps you see the events from outside and think about them slightly less emotionally. Tell the story in whatever way you want.

2. If worries are keeping you awake, write them on paper (not a computer or other device). If you plan to do anything about these worries tomorrow you can write that down, too. Then fold the paper up and put it away from your bed. You can look at it in the morning but not before. Then get into bed, turn the light off and focus on one of the visualisation strategies on pages 103–4.

3. Try to feel that you have got something off your mind by putting it into written words. It's now less powerful in your mind.

4. You can choose to keep or destroy the written worries after you've finished writing them down.

WRITING STRATEGY 2 | WRITE A JOURNAL

Some people find this very helpful. It can help them feel grounded, present and safe, and they can focus their thoughts in a mindful way instead of having them spiral out of control.

WHAT TO DO

* You can use a blank book or buy a printed journal with ideas about what to include. These journals help if you find it hard to think of what to write, as they have boxes that suggest specific ideas. There might be emojis to choose from to express your feelings. There are journals for all ages, from young children to adults – find the one that's right for you!

* It's good to create a habit by writing at the same time each day. Just before you get into bed would be perfect. And it only needs to take a few minutes.

* Some days you might write hardly anything – or nothing. That's fine. It's your journal!

CAUTION

Some people do not find journalling helpful and it *can* make you feel worse. If you find that it makes you more anxious or upset, stop doing it for now. You might enjoy it later.

WRITING STRATEGY 3 | JUST WRITE!

When I was at school, I used to write gloomy poetry and stories. I enjoyed pushing my emotions to the limit in the safety of a made-up world. This can be good for anxiety because you can become completely engaged in it, so there's no headspace for other worries.

WHAT TO DO

1. **Decide what to write about before you sit down. Most people do not get ideas when they're in front of the paper or screen!**

2. **Find a time when you won't be disturbed. You might listen to music through headphones.**

3. **Just get some words down and don't judge them at first. Once you've started, you can either keep going or redraft.**

4. **Try to write for at least 25 minutes before stopping for a break or to redraft.**

5. **Be proud – you just put some words together in a completely original way!**

IDEAS TO START YOU OFF

* Write your own version of a poem or song you love.
* Tell a story or write a poem without using a particular letter.
* Pick a character from a book you enjoyed and write a new story for them.
* Write an alternative ending or sequel to a story you know.
* Write a story where you're the hero.
* Investigate fan fiction online.

TIP
Use the time when you're trying to sleep to get your ideas.

EXPRESS YOURSELF IN ART

If you think of yourself as artistic you probably already spend time drawing or doing some other kind of art. But if you don't think you're artistic, think again! There are lots of easy and fun ways that anyone can express themselves through visual creativity. And it's a great way to engage your mind away from your worries.

WHAT TO DO

1. **Super-doodling – doodling is when you casually decorate whatever piece of paper is in front of you (not this book, please!) Super-doodling (my invention!) is when you get a piece of blank paper and aim to fill the whole page with your doodling. Start in one corner, perhaps with a spiderweb or parallel wavy lines, and keep going until the page is filled. You could listen to music at the same time.**

2. **Colouring in – you probably did colouring in as a child. Nowadays lots of adults do it, too. You'll find colouring books or downloadable designs online.**

3. **Origami – making 3D figures using only paper is an ancient art and great fun to learn. Again, there are lots of resources online.**

4. **Design something on paper – an outfit, hairstyle, dream bedroom, treehouse, enormous ship, rocket. Let your imagination take off!**

COOK OR BAKE

Every great cook begins somewhere: following a recipe, making mistakes, having successes and not-so-successes. It can be a good way to deal with anxiety because it takes you away from your worries for a while as you have to focus on what you're doing.

WHAT TO DO

1. Decide what sort of thing you'd like to cook. It should be something you'd like to eat and something not too difficult at first. Discuss with the adults in your home to make sure the ingredients are available and the kitchen is free.

2. You might prefer to cook on your own, but do have an adult near by in case of a problem. And if you prefer to cook *with* someone, do it!

3. Read through the whole recipe at least twice. Get all your utensils and ingredients ready. Make sure you have enough time so you're not rushing: recipes always underestimate the amount of time needed because the writers forget that it can take a long time to find and weigh everything.

4. Ready, steady, cook!

READ FOR PLEASURE

Reading for pleasure improves knowledge and vocabulary, sparks ideas, builds empathy, raises self-esteem, widens the mind and reduces stress and anxiety.

While you're deep in a book you can't *also* be worrying about whatever was making you anxious. You have a break while you're reading – and you might forget your worries for a while afterwards, too. I even invented a word for this: "readaxation" means deliberately reading to relax. You'll find links in the Resources, including how to find the research into the benefits.

WHAT TO DO

1. Obviously, if you already love reading I don't need to tell you how to do it. Just do it – ideally just before you go to sleep.

2. If you're not a keen reader, I can help you. First, believe that it *will* make you feel better in so many ways. You could experiment and measure your anxiety each evening before and after reading. (You can download the "readaxation diary" from my website.)

3. Realise that you can choose any book you want. You can read something easy or funny or childish or disgusting – whatever you want, provided it's long enough to "get into".

4. If you can't find anything you like, ask your school librarian. They are BRILLIANT at helping individual readers choose.

5. Put your phone away and read for twenty minutes before bed. Reading helps you sleep.

WATCH A FILM OR TV

This is one of the easiest distractions there is – easier than reading for most people. It's hard to feel anxious when your mind is engaged in a film or TV programme. Do read all the points below, however, as there are some things to be careful about.

WHAT TO DO

1. Obviously, just find a film or show and watch it. But the following are important points.

2. Be careful about the emotions you might experience: if you're already feeling sad, don't watch a sad film; if supernatural stories make you afraid or disturb your sleep, steer clear of such themes; if you have an eating disorder, don't choose something that might trigger your anxiety around food.

3. It's best not to watch screens too close to bedtime, as they tend to make you alert or excited. Also, a film is usually long and could well occupy time when you should be sleeping. And, if you are watching online, it's too easy to carry on scrolling through more items offered to you. Switch off all notifications, as they are very unlikely to help your mental state.

4. Choose films appropriate for your age. Once you've seen something that shocks you, you can't "unsee" it.

5. Finally, make sure that you also have physical and social activities in your list of distraction strategies. You need a healthy variety of actions.

PLAY A COMPUTER GAME

Many people say they find gaming relaxing. What they usually mean is that they find it distracting. There are a few important things to think about.

BEFORE YOU START

1. You need to be able to stop when required, for meals or homework, for example. If you can't set limits, that is a problem.

2. You need other distraction activities too, including physical activity and face-to-face time.

3. Gaming must not get in the way of a healthy lifestyle: things like eating a balanced diet, drinking water, being active, being social, doing schoolwork and sleeping for around eight hours at night.

4. The gaming needs to create positive emotions: if it makes you anxious, irritable or dissatisfied, it's not helping you. And it could make your anxiety worse.

WHAT TO DO

1. Choose a game you believe will give you the right relaxation or distraction.

2. Set a time limit – no more than an hour – and use a timer.

3. Every few minutes, give your eyes a change by looking at things in the far distance.

4. Every 30 minutes, get up and move about.

5. Afterwards, do something completely different, ideally involving physical activity.

TIP

If you feel you can't control your gaming, it's affecting you negatively, or you're anxious about it, talk to a trusted adult who will understand and help find strategies.

OTHER DISTRACTIONS

Here are a few more distracting activities to choose from.

WHAT TO DO

1. **Any hobby – you might also find new friends and opportunities.**

2. **Laugh – this raises mood and lowers anxiety. You might not always feel like laughing but if you make a list of your favourite YouTube funnies you'll have something to make you smile.**

3. **Watch sport – if you support a team, watching them is a great way to distract you from your anxiety. But if you don't, there's always a competition to watch online somewhere. It could be gymnastics or synchronised swimming or anything where the skill level is mesmerising.**

4. **Learn a poem or song lyrics – this has the extra benefit of improving your memory and giving you some beautiful and meaningful words to inspire you.**

MANAGE YOUR MIND

Let's focus on your mind: your thoughts and feelings. Up to now I've been focusing on strategies that are to do with action – doing or not doing something. I started there because it's often easier and quicker to notice, deal with and change sensations in your body than it is to alter what happens in your mind. But your mind is where anxiety starts: with the thoughts, reactions or emotions that make you feel anxious or behave in a stressed way. You can't deal with anxiety without looking at your thoughts and emotions.

There are a lot of ideas coming up. You won't want – or be able – to do them all but some of them will jump out at you as being perfect for you. Some are really simple, others take more practice or might even need someone to help you learn them.

Most of the ideas are based around the principles of Cognitive Behavioural Therapy so the next page explains how this works.

COGNITIVE BEHAVIOURAL THERAPY (CBT)

"Cognitive" means "relating to what's in our mind": things like thoughts, beliefs, ideas. "Behavioural" means "relating to our behaviours and actions". "Therapy" means "a way of treating or healing". So, CBT is a form of treatment that involves looking at and, if necessary, changing thoughts and beliefs so that you behave, feel and think in a more useful and positive way.

For example, supposing you get very anxious about joining in with sport. Supposing this is because you don't like your body and you think everyone is judging you when you get changed. And supposing this leads you to avoid playing sport or going swimming, which is a negative result because sport and swimming are positive actions. In this case, CBT would help you find healthy ways of thinking so that you could feel less anxious about playing sport or going swimming. By altering your thoughts and beliefs, you'd alter your body's reactions, and this would alter how you behave, by making you less afraid and therefore better able to do the thing you fear.

CBT is probably the most common form of treatment for many sorts of mental health problem, including anxiety. It has a lot of trusted research behind it and is widely recommended by health professionals.

If you see a professional to help your anxiety, it is very likely they will use CBT. Some of the ideas that follow are very closely linked to CBT principles. All of the strategies have the same goal: to reduce your anxiety by helping you think in more positive and constructive ways.

JUST NOW

Whatever you're going through right now, how you feel is only how you feel *now*. Whether your anxiety is about something happening now, or something you worry might happen in the future, how you feel about it later will be different.

I have a very simple strategy to embed this idea. It's an incredibly powerful mental tool. If you try nothing else from this section, do this!

WHAT TO DO

1. **Whenever you're feeling anxious – or sad, fearful, angry, upset – add the words "just now" after (or before) your statement about how you feel. For example:**

   ✱ **"I am so worried about my exams" – "I am so worried about my exams just now".**

   ✱ **"I can't sleep" – "I can't sleep just now".**

   ✱ **"I feel worried and sick" – "I feel worried and sick just now".**

   ✱ **"I feel so angry with my mum/friend/teacher" – "I feel so angry with them just now".**

2. **Think about the words "just now". What do they mean? Only now. They remind us that emotions change: emotions are like water, travelling and flowing where it finds space. Now, the shape of the stream means that you feel anxious, sad, angry, but soon the shape and surroundings of the stream will change. The water keeps moving but it moves differently as it passes through different landscapes.**

3. **The phrase we sometimes use – though it's a bit old-fashioned – is "This, too, shall pass". Being old-fashioned doesn't make it wrong! It has stood the test of time and is as meaningful today as it was fifty or a hundred years ago. So, say this to yourself when you are feeling any strong and uncomfortable emotion.**

SPOT YOUR NEGATIVE THOUGHTS

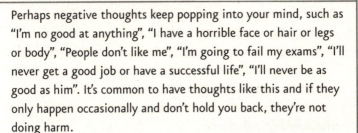

Perhaps negative thoughts keep popping into your mind, such as "I'm no good at anything", "I have a horrible face or hair or legs or body", "People don't like me", "I'm going to fail my exams", "I'll never get a good job or have a successful life", "I'll never be as good as him". It's common to have thoughts like this and if they only happen occasionally and don't hold you back, they're not doing harm.

If these thoughts happen often, if they make you feel rubbish and drag you down, or if they stop you grasping opportunities and aiming high, then such negative thoughts are a problem. But they are just your negative mind's opinion, not reality.

WHAT TO DO

1. Spend a few minutes thinking about what your typical negative thoughts are. How often do you have these thoughts? How big a problem do they seem? Are they holding you back? Do they stop you joining in or taking opportunities or succeeding?

2. Now take one of these thoughts and challenge it. What evidence supports it? Is it caused by your lack of self-esteem? If this negative belief just comes from your feelings about yourself, not evidence, how important should it be? If a comment from someone else has given you this negative idea, why have you believed them? Could they be wrong?

3. Work out how the thought makes you behave. Does it stop you "going for it"? Does it make you avoid certain things that could improve your life? If so, it would be worth trying to change the thought.

4. Look at the next two pages and work your way through the ideas.

REFRAME YOUR NEGATIVE THOUGHTS

Thoughts are just words in your head. Your brain makes them. Sometimes you let your brain behave as though you have no power over it. But you have! When negative thoughts come, you can reframe them. (You can also change or control them, as you'll see on the pages after this.)

WHAT TO DO

1. Recognise that thoughts are only words in your head and they are affected by your mood.

2. Change the words of your thoughts like this:

   * "I'm no good at this" becomes "my anxiety makes me feel…"

   * "I have a horrible face/legs/body" becomes "my low self-esteem makes me feel…"

   * "People don't like me" becomes "my low confidence makes me think…"

   * "I'm going to fail my exams" becomes "my anxiety makes me feel negative about exams" or "I am frightened that I might fail my exams".

   * "I'll never get a good job or have a successful life" becomes "my anxiety makes me worry about the future instead of focusing on working hard now".

   * "I'll never be as good as him" becomes "my habit of comparing myself with him makes me feel inadequate but if I focus on doing my best I'll achieve so much".

CHALLENGE YOUR ANXIOUS THOUGHTS

Is there something that often makes you anxious? Or something you are anxious about right now? Here is a strategy to challenge those anxious thoughts and put them in perspective.

WHAT TO DO

1. When you have one of your anxious thoughts, ask yourself these questions and think carefully about the answers:
   * What's the worst that could happen?
   * What would I need to do if it did? What would be the best actions?
   * Who would help me?
   * How likely is it that the worst thing will happen?
   * How much time would be sensible to spend thinking about it?

2. Let those thoughts pass through your mind before using one of the next two strategies.

3. If you are feeling anxious right now, try one of the anxiety-reducing Instant Actions from pages 77–92.

CHOOSE WHAT TO PAY ATTENTION TO

We can't pay attention to *everything* around us so we unconsciously filter it. Two people in the same situation will not pay attention to the same things and your mood strongly affects what you do or don't notice. And what you notice affects your mood. If you focus on negative things – such as sad, shocking or stressful news stories or worries about what might happen – those negative things will be loud in your mind: you'll pay even more attention to them.

But you *can* choose to pay attention to something else.

WHAT TO DO

When a negative, intrusive thought or idea tries to take over, give your mind another task. For example:

1. If you're outside, look for birds, trees or insects. Challenge yourself to find a certain number.

2. Pay attention to your breath, noting that you can slow it down or speed it up; feel it filling your lungs.

3. What shapes can you see in the clouds?

4. If you're outside in a town, how many different sorts of shop can you see?

5. Can you find four different species of tree in your neighbourhood? Do you know what they are called?

6. In your bedroom, can you find ten things to put away?

7. In your home, can you hear four different sounds?

8. Can you remember and write down the phone numbers of everyone in your household?

9. Write down a random ten-digit number and then learn it.

10. Learn the words of a song.

THOUGHT STOPPING

You have the power to stop negative thoughts dominating. Think of your mind as a house: you can't stop people ringing the bell, but you don't have to let them come in and cause trouble. Thought stopping involves making your negative thought stop advancing towards you. Like holding up your hand and saying: "Wait. Stop there."

However, before I show you how, please note that sometimes it's the wrong thing to do.

If you do it at the wrong times, what you're really doing is avoidance. And avoiding the thing we're afraid of makes the fear worse in the long run. I've mentioned this before, for example on pages 60–1 when I talk about negative coping strategies. See below for good times to use thought stopping, then try the ideas on the next page.

BEFORE YOU START

1. You can try thought stopping at times when you've got something important to do and your worries would prevent you getting your task done or enjoying some time out.

2. Another good opportunity is when you recognise a worry creeping up on you and you can use the "Stop" part of the START method (see page 76). You will be able to continue to tackle the worry, once you've halted it.

3. You could also practise thought stopping when you are trying to sleep.

In these cases, you are not running away from the worry: you are putting it in its place and intending to deal with it at a sensible time. You will deal with it at a time of your choice.

TIPS FOR THOUGHT STOPPING

Have you read the previous page? You're sure you wouldn't be running away from the worry? You'd be controlling it, not being controlled by it? Then here is a strategy you could try.

WHAT TO DO

1. When the negative thought arrives, decide which of these methods you fancy:

    a. Saying (out loud or in your head) "STOP". Say it firmly, as though you're in charge, which you are.

    b. Visualising a big red STOP sign or a locked gate.

    c. Visualising your guard dog growling at the thoughts. The guard dog is brilliantly trained by you and will do exactly as you say.

    d. Saying firmly but quietly, "Go away: negative thoughts are not welcome here right now."

2. Put a more positive thought in its place. This should be something relating to the worry. For example, if you're worried about failing an exam, your positive thought could be "I am going to do my best and that is all anyone can expect". This will start a new pathway in your brain – see page 137.

3. Be proud of yourself for what you just did: you prevented a negative thought dominating your mind.

TIP

If you like the idea of using humour to deal with a negative thought or worry, see the next page!

EYE-ROLL YOURSELF

When you say or do something and someone rolls their eyes at you, you feel humiliated, embarrassed, uncomfortable – yes? Well, what if you roll your eyes at your own anxious thought? You'd put the thought in its place, make it feel uncomfortable. It might not want to bother you again. Excellent!

BEFORE YOU START

★ This is only appropriate when the anxious thought is an unhelpful one, such as a familiar intrusive thought that keeps annoying you. If it's actually a valid one – such as when you're going into an exam – *don't* eye-roll yourself because a small amount of anxiety here is appropriate and useful.

WHAT TO DO

1. In your mind, say something like, "Here we go again – here comes that silly or annoying or pointless thought. What a waste of time it is!" Imagine rolling your eyes at it or shaking your head. You're not angry with it, just bored and uninterested.

2. Picture the thought looking funny. Maybe it's got a huge pink traffic cone on its head, or it's dressed like a scarecrow, or its skin is green with pink spots.

3. Wave it away – "Off you go – play somewhere else – I've got other things to do here."

4. Get on with whatever you actually want or need to focus on.

TIP

Remember that this shouldn't be used to avoid things you're afraid of. As with thought stopping, this is a temporary method of controlling what you pay attention to. When you need to deal with a fear, you can.

TALK TO YOURSELF

Everyone talks to themselves – mostly just in their head, although sometimes they might say something aloud. It can be whole conversations, either going over actual conversations or imagining future ones. Often it's just scattered thoughts: "I'm bored … I'd like a biscuit … I must remember to message Jo … I wonder if Mum will be home late tonight…"

Are the words in your head often self-critical? "Why did I do that? I'm an idiot. I should have concentrated. I get so nervous – it's ridiculous. Everyone is laughing at me. I'm so stupid. Why can't I be more like Serena or Sajid? They're so good at speaking in public and I'm so useless. I'm useless at everything."

Is that what you'd say to a friend if they were upset or worried? No! So, be a good friend to yourself.

WHAT TO DO

1. When you're having anxious or negative thoughts, think what you'd say to a friend in the same situation. Perhaps you'd say, "It was bad luck! Don't worry – everyone will forget and they'll think you're so brave if you try again. You could get tips from my mum – she used to find things like that difficult. Anyway, I wouldn't even be brave enough to have got up on stage – I was so proud of you!"

2. Remind yourself that you do have people on your side but the person who must have your back most of all is YOU.

3. Finish by saying, "I can do this."

BUILD A WORRY BOX

A worry box is where you put your worries so that you can think about them at a time of your choosing (which might be never). It can be an actual box or it can be inside your head. You can put your box in the bin any time you want!

WHAT TO DO

1. **Choose whether to have an actual box or an imaginary one. Design it however you want, as long as it has a lid. It could have words that express how you feel about worries, or it could be decorated with patterns that make you feel calm. Your choice!**

2. **If you have a real box, write your worries and put them inside.**

3. **If you have an imaginary box, *visualise* putting your worries in the box.**

4. **Close the lid of your box.**

5. **Choose whether to keep the lid on and leave the worries inside or take one out at a time of your choosing. If you take one out, give yourself a few minutes to worry about it. After you've done that, either tear it into tiny pieces (in reality or your imagination) and put it in the bin – or back in the box, if you want to worry about it again later.**

TIP

Think carefully whether you would want someone to read your worries. If you don't, it's best to keep your box imaginary.

SCHEDULE A TIME TO WORRY

When a worry keeps dominating or intruding, it can be a good idea to set aside a time for it – not to avoid it, but to control when you focus on it. That way you can pay appropriate attention to it but not let anxiety get in the way of your work, your leisure or your sleep.

WHAT TO DO

1. Look at your schedule for the next 24 hours and set aside a small amount of time to think about the worry. (Not when you're meant to be going to sleep!) Write the time down in your schedule or diary. If you worry that someone will see, give it a code, such as TTP (Tackle The Problem). Set an alarm on your phone, if you want.

2. Forget about it until the appointed time. If the thought tries to intrude earlier, do some thought stopping. On the other hand, if you find yourself with time to deal with it earlier than you planned, that's fine, as long as it's your choice. If something important crops up at your appointed time, you can reschedule.

3. When the time arrives, think about how you will approach the worry. You might use any of the strategies in the Manage Your Mind section (pages 124–47). Do you want to write some thoughts down? Perhaps you will think about how you might talk to someone else about your worry.

4. As you approach the end of the time slot, remind yourself, just like the end of a meeting or a lesson, that this slot is about to end so you will stop thinking about it. Let it go. Your job is done.

MAKE PATHWAYS IN YOUR MIND

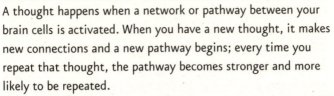

A thought happens when a network or pathway between your brain cells is activated. When you have a new thought, it makes new connections and a new pathway begins; every time you repeat that thought, the pathway becomes stronger and more likely to be repeated.

So, the more often a thought happens, the easier it is to have the thought. It becomes automatic. That's great if the thought is "I'm good at this" but not if the thought is "No one likes me". It's great if the thought is "Copenhagen is the capital of Denmark" but not if the thought is "Copenhagen is the capital of Norway".

Importantly, you can create new pathways, better pathways. Better thoughts.

WHAT TO DO

1. **Think the correct or desired thought. Often. Say it in your head.**

2. **Reinforce it by saying it aloud, writing it down – in different voices, colours, fonts. Soon you will know that Copenhagen is the capital of Denmark. And if you think "I am worthy, loved, capable" you will know that, too.**

3. **When the wrong or undesired thought tries to come back, use your thought-stopping powers and repeat the right thought again.**

TIP

I have a pathways PowerPoint presentation on my website – see the Resources at the back of this book. It will help you visualise how pathways are formed in your brain when you repeat things.

MANAGE A PHOBIA

If you ask for professional help for a phobia, a mind-based method called "exposure" or "systematic desensitisation" will almost certainly be used. This strategy can be for when you meet the thing you fear and are feeling very anxious (intervention) and to reduce the fear in the first place (prevention). Below is a basic way to do exposure for yourself, but you will probably need help from an expert. Your doctor can help you find someone.

You will need a breathing strategy from pages 78–85. Practise it before you start this activity.

WHAT TO DO

1. **Think what exposure you could possibly try. For example, if your phobia is about spiders, could you look at a photo? Maybe a distant image? A small one?**

2. **While looking at it, use your breathing strategy to control your fear response. Focus on your breathing and notice your anxiety reduce. Notice how you can look at the picture and stay in control. Say the word "spider" a few times while focusing on breathing. This will reduce your fear response bit by bit.**

3. **Practise with the same photo or other exposure a few times for two or three days. It will be a little easier each time.**

4. **Introduce a slightly harder task – perhaps a bigger picture, a bigger spider. Use your anxiety-reducing strategy.**

5. **Gradually increase the exposure until you can cope with being quite close to – even touching – your feared object.**

6. **Be proud of any improvement. Your brain has learnt to deal with something that had previously distressed you.**

> **TIP**
> Avoidance does not help reduce a phobia. If you find yourself using avoidance a lot, you would benefit from help.

THINK POSITIVE

You can't change physical things in the world just by positive thinking, but there's a great deal you can do to change your thinking, and therefore your feelings, and therefore your anxiety. When you approach any situation, there are different ways your mind might be thinking. If you can push yourself to take a positive viewpoint you can give yourself more power, control, confidence and courage. And less anxiety.

For some people in some situations, this could simply be a matter of telling themselves to "be positive". But very often this is more difficult than it sounds.

The best and easiest way to switch your mind to a positive way of thinking is to do some practical actions, things that will help you approach a situation more confidently and with more power. The next four pages give you exactly such practical strategies.

LIST (OR DRAW) YOUR HAPPY

This is a useful and fun way to focus your thoughts more positively.

WHAT TO DO

1. Choose whether to do this on a notebook or scrap of paper or a bigger poster. Use coloured pens if you like.

2. In the middle of your paper, draw a smiley face. Add details to make it represent you. It needs a big smile on it, even if you don't feel smiley right now.

3. On the rest of the page, write or draw everything you can think of that makes you happy, everything that you like. Think of things that you sometimes do (even if you can't do them right now), as well as foods, colours, people, animals, films, favourite objects.

4. At first, you might find it hard to think of things. Let your mind search your world for everything you can think of that makes you happy.

5. Spend some time thinking about what you've put on the paper. There's a lot of happy there. Focus on your feelings and feel your smile grow.

WHAT WENT WELL?

This activity has lots of research behind it. It's sometimes called "three blessings" and comes from Martin Seligman, a founder of the "positive psychology" movement. Positive psychology looks at how psychology can prevent problems rather than wait until mental illness comes. That seems an obvious idea but it wasn't widely understood before.

WHAT TO DO

1. Each evening, set aside time for this. You could do it alone or with members of your family – maybe a dinner-time activity – or friends online. Maybe start a "what went well?" group?

2. Write three things that were good about your day. Think about:
   * Anything you're proud of, such as working or listening well.
   * Any happy thoughts about past, present or future.
   * Something delicious you ate.
   * Anything nice someone said to you.
   * Any reassurance someone gave you about a worry.
   * Any good news about yourself or someone close to you.

3. When you've written three things, take a moment to think about them and remember the happy feelings.

4. Do the activity on the next page!

KNOW YOUR PERSONAL QUALITIES

As well as the "What went well" activity, Martin Seligman also developed the idea of "character strengths". These are the personal qualities that help you achieve success in whatever is important to you.

In the Resources section of this book, you'll find a website with 24 character strengths and a quiz for you to assess yours. But here's how you can value your personal qualities even more simply.

WHAT TO DO

1. Look back at the three things you wrote for the activity on the previous page.

2. Think about what mental skills or actions you used to make these things happen or to notice and appreciate them. Did you work hard and were you determined? Did you listen carefully? Were you resilient or brave? Did you use curiosity? Did you use self-control to put your phone away and do your homework? Or to avoid doing something wrong? Did you use kindness, empathy or social skills? Did you appreciate and feel grateful for tasty food?

3. List other personal qualities you feel you have, not just the ones you used today. For example, how would you complete these: "I am good at..." or "I feel confident in..." or "I would love people to notice that I..."?

4. Be proud!

TIP

Although some of your qualities might seem "fixed" and hard to change, there's a lot you can do to build them and use them even better than you do now. And it all begins with recognising your qualities!

POSITIVE WORDS AND IMAGES

Words and images have enormous power over our minds. If you spend a lot of time reading, hearing or thinking about negative words, phrases or stories and seeing upsetting and negative images or scenes, your mood will inevitably be dragged downwards.

Fortunately, there's a simple, effective and free solution. You just have to choose to take it.

WHAT TO DO

1. **Make a list of words or phrases that are positive or things that you like. Put them on a poster to display in your room or just write them on your phone or somewhere you'll see them often. Here are some suggestions:**

   ★ **I'm a good person.**

   ★ **I am determined, valuable, hard-working.**

   ★ **I love…**

   ★ **I'm proud of…**

   ★ **I can do this.**

   ★ **Chocolate, sunshine, holidays, pizza, friends, birthdays, blue sky, seaside, the moon, reading a book, a hug.**

2. **Say them any time you notice your mood becoming negative or anxious.**

3. **Find photos and images that make you smile. Save them on your phone in a folder and give it a name such as "happy pics".**

4. **Look at these images several times a day. As you look at them, spend some time allowing your mind to absorb the happy feelings from those images.**

THINK BACK

Often we forget that feelings come and go, and that our worries of last year – or last month – have faded. It's good to remember that bad feelings fade.

WHAT TO DO

1. Think back to a year ago – or two years or five or however many you want. Or just think back to a difficult time. What were you worried about?

2. What was that like at the time? Try to recall your thoughts: the words in your head, what you said to yourself. How strong or painful were your feelings or emotions? Did you find it hard to think of anything else?

3. How do you feel about that worry now? Does it seem quite far away, quite blunt or dull? That's what happens to feelings: they become weaker and lose their power to hurt. Sometimes that happens quickly and sometimes more slowly, but it happens. Not always completely but sometimes that, too.

4. Use this knowledge to think about what you're worried about now. Remind yourself that one day you won't feel so bad, anxious or distressed.

THINK FORWARD

This is a great exercise when you're anxious about something coming up, such as an exam, performance, presentation. It's what I do every time I'm nervous about a speech or an event that I know is going to be difficult, stressful or important.

WHAT TO DO

1. **Think ahead to when the event is finished. Focus on a specific time, such as that evening or the next day or even just five minutes after. How will you feel and what will you do to celebrate or acknowledge that you got through it?**

2. **Use the time before the event to make sure you've done what you can to give it your best shot. Do you need to do something to make you feel calmer? (Try the Instant Actions on pages 77–92.) Or do you need food or drink for energy? Do you need to check something or ask your teacher a question? Do you need to talk to an adult or friend about anything? Doing something practical to prepare for the event will make you feel better in control.**

3. **If you've done all the preparation you can, now choose a relaxation activity and something to distract you if you need that. And keep reminding yourself how great you'll feel when it's over and you've done your best job.**

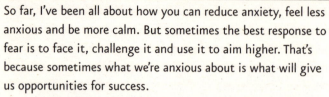

FACE YOUR FEAR

So far, I've been all about how you can reduce anxiety, feel less anxious and be more calm. But sometimes the best response to fear is to face it, challenge it and use it to aim higher. That's because sometimes what we're anxious about is what will give us opportunities for success.

I'm not talking here about general anxieties about illness, or loss, or any of the "what ifs" that we sometimes waste time worrying about. We can't do anything about them. I'm talking about things which are positive but scary. Examples might be trying out for a team, auditioning for the school play, choosing to present your ideas in an assembly, aiming for a difficult college course, applying to be a prefect or head student. Here are some good ways to face these common experiences.

WHAT TO DO

1. **Think what you will gain if you succeed. And what you will gain if you don't succeed. This will help you see the point of trying.**

2. **Now think how you will feel coming up to this event. Acknowledge the thoughts, effort, emotions and physical signs of anxiety that you might have to deal with. This is part of your preparation.**

3. **Decide how you will deal with those things. Which strategies from this book will you use?**

4. **Focus on preparing for the challenge itself: what work will you need to put in? What will give you the best chance of success? Whose help might you need? Whose support do you want?**

5. **Finally, whatever happens, be proud of yourself for tackling your anxiety head-on. You will now be able to do it again, and again, and again. And sometimes you will succeed and that feeling will be brilliant!**

HARNESS YOUR SPIRITUAL BELIEF

Many people are comforted by spiritual or religious faith. Research supports the idea that this can benefit mental and physical health. (The Resources section has a link to some research on this.) "Spiritual belief" is one of the character strengths that Martin Seligman identified (see page 142).

If you don't have such faith – as I don't – don't worry: there are plenty of other ways to reach an accepting and calm way of being. Just as mindfulness doesn't work for everyone, nor does religion. You are not a bad person if they don't work for you.

If you do have spiritual faith, it is worth seeing how it might help you feel less anxious or put your worries in context.

WHAT TO DO

1. Start by talking to a trusted teacher in the faith you are part of. Tell them you often feel anxious and ask how you can deal with this.

2. Remind yourself that most faiths hold that there is a higher being who leads you. You place yourself in the hands of this being. This removes some responsibility from you and reminds you that there are things you can't control. When you pray, you are asking for help.

3. Choose your favourite calming quote from any faith and make a poster. Here's one, called the Serenity Prayer: "God, grant me the serenity to accept the things I cannot change, courage to change the things I can, and wisdom to know the difference." You don't have to be religious to find truth in this, but if you are you might find extra power in it.

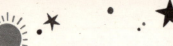

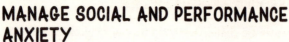

MANAGE SOCIAL AND PERFORMANCE ANXIETY

On page 56 I talked about social anxiety, which can either be mild (which is very common indeed) or more severe, sometimes enormously affecting your ability to function well around other people. Even if you don't have a diagnosis of this disorder, it's incredibly common – almost universal – to feel uncomfortable in situations where you feel you are being looked at. This applies to both social situations and times when you have to "perform" in front of other people, whether taking part in a social or group activity, asking or answering questions in front of others, or giving a presentation or speech or other sort of performance.

Whether you experience this anxiety very strongly or mildly, and whether you feel this is a major problem in your life or just an occasional feeling of discomfort, the advice on the next pages will help you.

If you find social or performance situations so distressing that they are spoiling your ability to thrive at school or in your social life, do seek further help. You could start with the Resources at the back of this book.

One thing is for sure: avoiding social or performance situations is not a good idea. You certainly don't have to become a professional performer if you don't want to, but being able to cope when you have to speak up or be seen is an extremely empowering life skill.

So, read on for some strategies to help you find these situations easier.

SMALL STEPS TO MAKING FRIENDS

On page 113, I gave you some ideas for being social. But what if those things seem too hard, as they might well do if you suffer very much from social anxiety? Here are some ideas for taking steps towards feeling more confident and less anxious about engaging with other people.

WHAT TO DO

1. **Ask a question.** This takes the pressure off you for a few moments and the other person will probably be happy that you showed an interest. It could be "Where did you get your top?", "Do you like…?", "What do you think of…?", "Did you see…?"

2. **Play a board game.** This means you don't have to make conversation because the game creates the content of your time with the other person.

3. **Instead of going to someone's house for a chat,** which can be daunting if you don't feel good at chatting, suggest a walk or a visit somewhere, such as a shopping centre or park. When you're doing things like this, you don't have to keep the conversation going all the time.

4. **Compare opinions about something easy** such as music tastes, films or shows you like.

5. **If you sense that someone else is also quiet and finds social situations daunting,** see if you can find a way to support each other. Agree to arrive at events together. Set each other small challenges.

6. **Set yourself small challenges!** It could be: ask the shop assistant a question about an item. Ask the way somewhere. Smile and say hello to someone on their own at school. Ask a teacher how they are.

TIPS FOR DEALING WITH INTROVERT ANXIETY

An introvert is someone who usually finds social interaction more tiring and stressful than extroverted people do. Introverts are extra sensitive to noise and people and are more likely to worry what people think and to be socially anxious. So, some situations – and this very much applies to school because school is full of noise and people – are an extra challenge for introverts.

Your introversion is valuable: it helps you be sensitive to others, a deep thinker, empathetic, a respected leader and wonderful team member. But you might need some extra help to feel less anxious in social situations.

WHAT TO DO

1. **Learn about introversion so you understand it better and properly value your personality. You'll find some help in the Resources at the end of this book.**

2. **Don't avoid all opportunities to be social but do be selective. For example, you might be better doing something with one or two people rather than in a large group, so it's OK *sometimes* to say no to something with a group.**

3. **Be open: explain to your friends that sometimes you just want to be alone – there's nothing wrong with them or you. (It's most likely that some of the people around you feel the same.)**

4. **Accept that you will feel anxious when speaking up in front of others; accept it as natural and your brain's way of helping you think carefully before speaking, which is not a bad thing. Practise your breathing skills to reduce this anxiety and keep your guard dog in check.**

5. **Be proud of yourself every time you do manage to speak up and join in well.**

6. **Build quiet time into your life. You probably can't get this at school but make sure your evenings and weekends contain enough time alone to recharge your batteries.**

SEE THROUGH OTHERS' EYES

We think we know what someone else is thinking when they are watching us. Often we will be wrong. And very often we think they are seeing us far more negatively than they are.

In reality, other people are mostly not looking at you, or irritated by you, laughing at you, thinking badly of you. They might be occasionally; after all, sometimes you are thinking such things about them. But then you move on and think about something else. Like you, other people have lots of different things on their minds. It's not always about you!

If you spend a lot of time worrying what people are thinking, try these suggestions.

WHAT TO DO

1. **Try to act in ways that make *you* proud, not to impress others. Then people who care about you will be proud of you, too. They are the ones who matter.**

2. **Remember that the person you think is looking at you also has thoughts and worries of their own, and lots to pay attention to. If you think you've done something embarrassing, they've probably forgotten – if they even noticed.**

3. **Don't take yourself too seriously. If you're worried about people looking at you, say to yourself, "There I go again, taking myself too seriously!"**

4. **Focus on what you're going to do next, not what you've just done.**

5. **How people see you will change, so if you've messed up and people are seeing that, they'll also see what you do next – and that could be brilliant.**

6. **Put on your best smile! A simple smile is an incredibly powerful way to encourage people to think warmly and positively about you.**

151

SHELTER IN A GROUP

Although you might find it a scary thought, being in a group of people can be really helpful for a quiet or shy person. In a group, you are not – or do not have to be – the centre of attention. You can blend in and let others do the talking. The others will appreciate you for just being there and supporting them.

Group activities can also help take your mind off your worries because you have to concentrate on what you're doing, not what you're thinking. But how to take the plunge and join in in the first place?

WHAT TO DO

1. When there's any opportunity to join in, try to say yes even if part of you wants to say no. Ask yourself, "What benefits might happen if I do this?"

2. If you know someone else is going to the same activity, suggest going together. People are usually very happy to be asked. They might be nervous, too!

3. If you're anxious about a social activity, tell an adult that you want to do it but you're feeling anxious. They can encourage you.

4. Think about activities that aren't connected with school. For example, could you join a climbing class or a film club?

5. Remember that quiet people are just as valuable and successful as noisy people. But sometimes we have to push ourselves a bit harder to make an effort to connect with others. There are people just like you, waiting to meet you!

> **TIP**
> "See through others' eyes" on the previous page has some more tips about this.

SPEAK EARLY

This is a great strategy for those situations where you feel you ought to contribute but you're really nervous about speaking up. Perhaps you're in class and your teacher expects each student to speak. Or perhaps you have to say something as part of an assignment or coursework assessment. But you're anxious about it and you find yourself sweating and displaying all the signs of anxiety. Here's something to try.

WHAT TO DO

1. **Make a decision that you're going to get your question or comment in early. Perhaps you'll even be the first to speak. Think how great you'll feel if you do this.**

2. **As you get ready to speak or put your hand up, notice any signs of anxiety and tell yourself, "This is just my body reacting to this situation. It's quite normal. I'm stepping up to a challenge."**

3. **Put into action your favourite breathing and grounding strategies.**

4. **As soon as you feel yourself becoming a little more in control, take a good breath in and take your turn. Don't wait too long: you can still do this even if you're feeling anxious.**

5. **It almost doesn't matter what you say – it's the fact that you said it that counts most. Once you've spoken, use your breathing or other strategies again while you recover. Be proud that you did it and try to relax now. Spend time listening to others and taking part by nodding or reacting in whatever way you feel is right.**

6. **You might even feel able to speak again!**

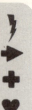

TIPS FOR GIVING A TALK OR PRESENTATION

Most people worry about public speaking. Many people absolutely hate it. But it's a very useful skill and the more you do it, the easier it gets. Luckily, there are lots of ways to reduce your anxiety and make it less uncomfortable.

WHAT TO DO

1. **Prepare and practise as well as you can. Practising aloud will really help. You don't have to do it in front of a mirror: practising saying the words is the main thing, so they become familiar. But they don't have to be learnt by heart; it often sounds better and more natural when they're not.**

2. **If using notes, use bullet points rather than the exact words. If you write the exact words, you risk either staring at them or losing your place when you look up. A list of bullet points is usually best. Make them easy to read, with a clear font at the right size.**

3. **If allowed, wear clothes you'll be comfortable and confident in and that won't show sweat.**

4. **Before your speech, use a breathing strategy to reduce anxiety. Sip water.**

5. **In the final seconds before you start, breathe slowly and moisten your mouth.**

6. **Look at the audience, relax your facial muscles and smile as though you're happy to be there. Even if you're not!**

7. **Keeping your chin up, speak more slowly than usual. This will also help your mouth not become dry. Push your voice out – you want them to hear every word!**

8. **Notice what you did well and what you'd do differently next time. You're learning! Next time will be a tiny bit easier. And the next time even more so.**

MORE TIPS FOR PUBLIC SPEAKING

The advice on the previous page is helpful for anyone but perhaps you'd like a bit more guidance? I have some ideas.

WHAT TO DO

1. **Do a presentation with someone else.** This is a brilliant way to practise public speaking because for half the time you will be experiencing some anxiety but not actually having to do anything – the spotlight isn't on you but you're there. During that time, you have the chance to get your breathing, heart rate and other signs of anxiety under control. You get the chance to practise dealing with anxiety without also having to perform. When it's your turn, you'll be ready to perform. The more times you can do this, the better practised you'll become. You'll soon be ready to present on your own.

2. **Make the audience do something.** If you ask them a question, or to write something down, or to turn to their neighbour and discuss a particular question, this takes the spotlight off you for a few moments. It gives the audience a bit of pressure and you a bit less! You could even just say "Hands up anyone who..." That can often be enough to enable you to feel more relaxed. It's also engaging for the audience.

3. **Is there something about the topic that would work if you told a story – made-up or true?** Start with this. This is a great way to relax you into the talk and stories are often easier to remember – for you and for the audience.

4. **Be true to yourself.** If you're not a natural comedian, do not feel you have to be funny! If you like to walk around, walk around and if you don't, don't. Don't feel you have to be like someone else – what works for them might not work for you. Find your style.

MANAGE YOUR WORK AND TIME

Having too much work and not enough time is a very common cause of anxiety. That worry of not being able to meet all your deadlines dominates your mind. I am very familiar with this myself! This sort of anxiety can also stop you sleeping: you lie awake worrying about everything you have to do and wondering how you can do it.

Anxiety about lack of time even comes within a special category of stress, called "scarcity". (I've included a book on this in the Resources.) Scarcity describes how, when you don't have enough time, resources, money or food, a lot of your attention or brain bandwidth is occupied by worrying about it. This makes you perform less well and make more mistakes.

The next few pages give you strategies especially for anxiety about not having enough time.

You will also benefit from the other anxiety-reducing strategies in this book.

The strategies on these pages are neither relaxing nor distracting, just sensible ways to deal with having too much to do, and therefore to reduce anxiety.

CHANGE YOUR BALANCE

One strategy that will work in some cases is to look at all the things that take up your time. If you changed any of them, would that improve how you feel?

WHAT TO DO

1. **List everything that will occupy time each day over the next week or two – whatever period of time you are worried about. Include schoolwork, social time and healthy lifestyle activities, as well as travelling, meals and breaks: everything that does or should occupy your time.**

2. **Split your list into things that take: less than 30 minutes a day; between 30 minutes and two hours; and more than two hours.**

3. **Now put everything into these categories: *must* do, really want to do, and could cut or postpone.**

4. **Discuss with a friend or an adult, explaining that you want to reduce your tasks. Sometimes, other eyes can see opportunities.**

5. **Think how you could reduce social media time and any time you feel is "wasted". This doesn't mean avoiding such activities altogether – we need fun! But be honest about how long they take and how you could get more work done in less time so you can relax.**

6. **Write your ideas into a plan. You do not need big changes.**

7. **Ask your friend or adult to help you put this into action.**

TIP

You will be able to do more than you think. Look ahead to the time when you'll be through this busy patch; take opportunities to look after yourself. And tell the adults in your life about the problem. Don't let overwork make you ill.

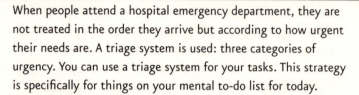

TASK TRIAGE

When people attend a hospital emergency department, they are not treated in the order they arrive but according to how urgent their needs are. A triage system is used: three categories of urgency. You can use a triage system for your tasks. This strategy is specifically for things on your mental to-do list for today.

WHAT TO DO

1. **Write down everything you believe you should do today. Include things that don't *have* to be done but you'd like to do.**

2. **In pencil, give each item an A, B or C, as follows:**
   - ★ **A = absolutely must be done today.**
   - ★ **B = ideally should be done today.**
   - ★ **C = nice to get done today but not vital.**

3. **Give each task the letter L for large or S for small. You can have M for medium too, if you want! Base this on how long it will take, not how difficult or important it is.**

4. **Look at your A items. Is it possible to do them all today? If not, you must first tell a relevant person that you're struggling but you'll try; or ask for help. If it's possible, get comfortable, put music on if you want to, and throw yourself into the first task.**

5. **Do one or two small items first. This gives you a sense of achievement. But don't leave all the large ones to last, as this can increase your anxiety.**

6. **If you can, after one or two A items, do one or two B items and a C – you'll feel satisfied! But don't worry if you can't – they're not necessary.**

TIP

If you find you cannot do what you're being asked to do each day, tell a relevant adult. You are human, not superhuman.

TIME MANAGEMENT

How often have you planned to do your homework and then lost all your time to social media? Or spent far too long on one task and had no time for the rest? This does not mean you lack self-discipline. It just means you didn't have a sensible plan or you didn't give yourself a chance to carry out your intentions.

I'll talk more about avoiding distractions, including your phone, on the next pages, but for now let's look at making a plan for your work session.

WHAT TO DO

1. Before you start work, write down the two to three main things you need to do, and any small things. Decide how long each should take. Make a timetable, with each big thing separated by a few minutes on small things. If it looks unmanageable, decide which tasks are most important. If you can't do them, you can't – just work as well as you can.

2. Get a snack and drink of water; get comfortable. Make sure everyone in your home knows not to disturb you. Maybe put a sign on the door? Make sure you can't receive notifications and put your phone out of sight and switched off.

3. Set a timer for the end of the first task. (Try the "Pomodoro technique" on page 161.)

4. If your attention wanders, pull it back on to the task. Don't beat yourself up – minds wander!

5. When the timer goes, feel proud of what you've achieved. If you haven't finished the task, still stick to your timetable.

> **TIP**
> Read the next pages for more time management tips. You need to find the ones that work for you.

PREPARE TO AVOID DISTRACTIONS

Your brain is wired to be easily distracted. Self-control is not the main answer; preparation and action are. Try these ideas.

WHAT TO DO

1. Think what is likely to distract you. Notifications? Temptation to check your phone for messages? Noise around you – someone else in the house? Thoughts in your head? Things you can see out of the window?

2. Before you start work, take actions to make those distractions as unlikely as possible. For example, put your phone out of the room; switch off all software or devices you're not using; use headphones and play familiar music to give yourself that sense of being in your own space. Make these actions a habit before every work session.

3. Use a timer to tell you when you can take a break and enjoy a short distraction. (And a timer to end that break...) See the next page for advice about the "Pomodoro technique".

4. Consider a blocking app to prevent you accessing the internet or social media while you're working. Options change all the time but an internet search should find a free one. Or your parents or carers might agree to a paid subscription for the household.

TIP

It really does help you get work done if you choose to restrict your access to devices and the internet. And it's amazingly satisfying and relaxing after a while.

POMODORO TECHNIQUE

A pomodoro is a mechanical kitchen timer shaped like a tomato. But there's nothing special about tomatoes (except that they taste nice) and you can use any timer at all!

The theory is that when we set a timer for 25 minutes and then allow ourselves a five-minute break, we concentrate better. It doesn't have to be 25 minutes but that's usually an amount which does not feel too much but is enough to get into a task. What often happens is that at the end of 25 minutes you want to carry on working. That's a great feeling.

WHAT TO DO

1. Get a timer – you can use your phone IF you turn off other notifications and remember that a phone is distracting itself. Online you'll find various free add-ons for your computer. A simple mechanical kitchen timer is great, too.

2. Get ready. Make sure you've got your timetable from page 159 and everything you need for your work session. Close all websites, software and pages that you won't be using.

3. Set the timer for 25 minutes or however long seems good to you.

4. Work! No distractions until the timer sounds. Then you can have a five-minute break, again using the timer. The best thing to do in your break is go for a brisk walk – round the house if necessary but outside is even better.

5. Then do another 25-minute work session. Each one is a "pomodoro" – see how many you do in a day. Be proud of each pomodoro!

DITCH TO-DO LISTS

I used to live by lists. But there's a problem with to-do lists, so now I only make lists that are NOT to-do lists. (For example, shopping, people to invite to a party, books I want to read.)

What's wrong with to-do lists? First, they don't distinguish between tiny and huge tasks: a to-do list for me might contain "order ink" (tiny) and "edit next book" (huge). They also don't tell me when I should do things (today? By Christmas?). The list can be enormous and terrifying; and I keep adding to it so it's endless.

So how do I remember my tasks? My method is based on "Getting Things Done", developed by productivity expert David Allen. You'll find more in the Resources, but here's the basic strategy.

WHAT TO DO

1. **Print weekly calendar templates – there are free ones online. Even better, use an app. (Search "productivity tools + getting things done".) You could use an ordinary online calendar, giving tasks a different colour from appointments. The main thing is that you need a place to put tasks in particular dates, not just a list.**

2. **When you think of a task, put it in your calendar.**

3. **Every single task, small or big, should have a date. If on paper, use a pencil so you can make changes. An app lets you move things whenever you want.**

4. **Each day, you look at your calendar to see what you have to do that day. You will never again see a huge scary list of tasks.**

TIP

If you use an app and you also have an online calendar such as iCalendar or Google Calendar, your app will sync with the calendar, which is even better.

BREAK THE TASK DOWN

If one of your tasks is "revise history" or "write essay on immigration", that task will probably feel very daunting or overwhelming. It's hard to know where to start. If that is making you feel anxious, break it down into the separate steps you need to take and when you'll do them.

So, although one of my tasks at the moment is "write book", what I actually write down as tasks in my calendar would be things like "write chapter one" or "check references". Here's how you could apply this to any big task you have.

WHAT TO DO

1. **Make a list of everything you need to do to complete this task. For example, for an essay, you'd need to do the following: plan the structure, locate the resources such as books or websites, make notes, write the first draft, redraft, redraft, proofread.**

2. **Put the list into the order of how you will do it.**

3. **Use your calendar template or app to find a suitable timeslot for each step.**

TIP

This works for pretty much any daunting task and it sounds very simple. And it *is* simple, but you might sometimes need another pair of eyes to help you work it out! Never let anxiety about a task overwhelm you: take a few calming breaths and face the task step by step.

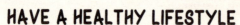

HAVE A HEALTHY LIFESTYLE

You might be surprised to discover just how much difference a generally healthy lifestyle makes to your anxiety levels. The strategies that follow will make you feel mentally and physically stronger, give you a sense of power and control over your life, and provide your body and brain with all the nutrients they need to function well.

The trouble is that when you feel worried, distressed and nervous, it's very easy to make the wrong choices – to reach for sugary treats, to have a poor bedtime routine, to scroll on social media instead of getting out and breathing in the fresh air or having fun with friends.

But a healthy lifestyle is not difficult and it has quick results. First you need to know what the healthy choices are and then you need a bit of help to make the choices easier for yourself. You also need to understand that these healthy choices will hugely benefit your anxiety levels. Believe me – they will!

So, now let's look at what those choices are and see how you can build them into your life.

> ## IMPORTANT NOTE ABOUT EXERCISE
> Make sure you're not doing too much exercise or feeling obsessed about it. If anyone suggests that you might be, discuss with an adult. Over-exercising or exercise obsession can be part of an eating disorder, especially if you are also wanting to lose weight. If you genuinely do need to lose weight in order to be healthier, a medical expert should tell you so.

GET PHYSICAL

Physical activity is medicine for the body and mind and can have an instant effect on anxiety, as well as a long-term one. It uses up cortisol, one of the stress hormones. It triggers endorphins, the body's "happy chemicals". And knowing that you did something good for you makes you feel proud afterwards.

This is a hard message for people who find exercise difficult or unpleasant. That's why I don't call it "exercise" but "being physically active". It needn't be "sport", or competitive or painful, and you do not have to be sweaty or out of breath. You can do it on your own, if you want. The next pages have some ideas.

If you have a disability that prevents you from joining in some of the ideas I'm going to suggest, please just focus on what you *can* do and make any adaptations you need.

WHAT TO DO

1. **Aim for at least 30 minutes of continuous activity a day. If you do an hour one day you can do less the next day.**

2. **If you are able to stand, avoid sitting for too long. Get up regularly and move about for a few minutes in any way you are able.**

3. **Vary your movement. Different activities strengthen legs, arms, or abdominal muscles; things that make you a bit out of breath are good for heart fitness. Activities such as yoga can be more relaxing, while others, such as football, are more distracting. Doing a variety of activities means you'll use more of your body and you won't over-exercise one part.**

4. **Don't feel you *"should"* like one particular thing. Just as with books, food and films, everyone has different tastes. But there *is* something for you. Read the next few pages for ideas.**

RELAXING PHYSICAL ACTIVITIES

Here are some ideas that are relaxing, though they might also be distracting when you have to concentrate hard. To learn how to do them, check out your local library for a class, or look for online videos. I've also put a few ideas in the Resources. And don't worry: everyone begins as a beginner!

WHAT TO DO

1. **Yoga** – stretches and poses to build strength, balance, flexibility and calmness. A class is useful at first so that you get the basics, but then it's definitely something you can do in private if you prefer. There is equipment but you can use household items.

2. **T'ai chi** – a Chinese martial art for defence rather than attack, but mostly used to achieve calmness and physical strength. As with yoga, you can learn online or in classes. People often do t'ai chi outside but you don't have to. No equipment is needed.

3. **Pilates** – strength-building movements which appear small and easy but all the work is going on in your core muscles. It's great for strength in all abdominal areas, pelvis, back, legs and hips. As with yoga and t'ai chi, it can be both relaxing and distracting, involving breath and focus.

4. **Stretching and strengthening** – if you don't want to learn any of the above, you can make your own stretching routine. Search online for stretching exercises or workouts and build your own set to do each day.

DISTRACTING PHYSICAL ACTIVITIES

If your chosen physical activity uses lots of concentration, it is likely to be distracting, rather than relaxing. The following physical activities are ones which raise your heart rate, so you can't literally feel relaxed during them. But you can feel happy, excited, eager, brave and proud – and those are all good for anxiety! And *afterwards* you can feel genuinely relaxed.

WHAT TO DO

1. An organised sport, as a team or in pairs – this can be a great way to find a new interest, friends and skills, all while improving fitness and reducing anxiety. It could be football, basketball, tennis, badminton – anything! You can join a group or class or just play with friends. Consider asking your school PE teachers for ideas and opportunities.

2. Something you can choose to do alone or with others – examples are swimming, running, climbing on a climbing wall, dancing to music in your room, fitness workouts online.

3. Geocaching or orienteering – you'd need to do this with other people. Check online for opportunities near you. It doesn't matter that most of the time you won't be out of breath: it's still a physical activity and great fun.

4. Join a class – some examples are dance fitness, gymnastics, yoga. Doing a class helps motivate many people and it can be a weekly thing to look forward to.

TIP

Going for a brisk walk is also brilliant exercise but it isn't usually distracting, because you still have headspace to think about any worries.

THINGS THAT DON'T FEEL LIKE AN ACTIVITY

You might be surprised how often you're already moving your body! Which of these things do you do already? Which could you do more of?

WHAT TO DO

1. Walk to school – or part of the way.
2. Take the stairs instead of a lift or escalator.
3. Walk up and down a flight of stairs or do ten star jumps between each work task or each online activity.
4. Dance to music in your room.
5. Offer to do the vacuuming.
6. Tidy your room as fast as you can.
7. Offer to sweep up leaves.
8. Go to the shops for your grandparents or a neighbour.
9. Bake bread – great for the arms!
10. Practise cartwheels.

MAKE GOOD FOOD CHOICES

Anxiety and food choices are a two-way thing: anxiety affects food choices and food choices affect anxiety.

Why does anxiety affect food choices? One reason is that worries occupy a lot of attention or "brain bandwidth", which you need to make good decisions. Another reason is that when you're feeling down, you want comforting foods, which often have high sugar, fat or salt content, or are highly processed. (Those foods are absolutely fine occasionally.) Another reason is that anxiety can make you feel alternately nauseous and very hungry, so you might not have balanced meals. Finally, anxiety can make you sleep badly, which affects your hunger hormones and makes you eat more sugar, fat and highly processed foods the next day.

Why do food choices affect anxiety? If you eat a lot of sugar, your glucose level goes up and down quickly, which can make you feel jittery, sweaty or faint, and that can make you anxious. We also know that some nutrients affect mood: for example, some B-vitamins affect how your brain functions. And the only way to be sure of getting all nutrients is through a varied diet including plenty of different vegetables and wholegrains. Finally, there can be a psychological effect when you worry that you're not doing your best to look after your brilliant body and mind.

What to do? It's much simpler than you might think! Read on.

IMPORTANT

Don't think of certain foods as "bad" or "good". But do think of some choices as being better than others and do think of a good diet as being a varied and balanced one. And don't become obsessed: food is for fuel and it is also for fun.

WHAT NOT TO PUT INTO YOUR BODY

Some foods and drinks can increase the body's stress responses. If you are often anxious or jittery, it's worth thinking about whether you consume a lot of these and seeing what happens when you cut them out.

WHAT TO AVOID

1. **Caffeine – it raises the heart rate and makes you feel on high alert. It stays in the body for many hours and disrupts sleep. And it can be addictive.**

   ✱ **Caffeine is in most coffee and ordinary teas (including green tea but not most herbal or fruit teas); it's also in cola and energy drinks and chocolate and cocoa products. Avoid from lunchtime onwards. (In fact, many dietitians advise that young people do not drink caffeine at all, especially energy drinks.)**

2. **Too much added sugar. Some foods, such as fruit, are naturally sweet and there is no problem with eating these. The problem comes when sugar is added to products – often called "hidden sugar". There is often far more than you'd imagine: a can of baked beans, for example, might have as much as nine teaspoons of sugar!**

   ✱ **These foods usually have a lot of added sugar: sweets, cakes, biscuits, milkshakes and smoothies (check if sugar is added), fizzy drinks, sauces and ketchups, tinned fruit (unless it says "in water" or "in fruit juice"). You can always check the ingredients – they have to be listed in order of amount, so if sugar is near the top of the list, there's a lot of it.**

WHAT TO PUT INTO YOUR BODY

There are no magic anxiety-reducing foods, but there are foods which contain good amounts of nutrients which scientists believe are important for mental health and mood, including anxiety. All these foods are nutritious and knowing that you're doing a good job for your body can also help you feel less anxious.

Here are some ideas to try. See how many you can include in your diet over the next week.

WHAT TO TRY

* Avocadoes.
* Bananas.
* Brown rice, brown pasta.
* Cheese.
* Chicken or turkey.
* Dark green vegetables – broccoli, spinach, cabbage.
* Mangoes.
* Milk (dairy, oat, nut or soya).
* Nuts – almonds, brazil, walnuts.
* Oats.
* Oily fish: tuna, salmon, mackerel, sardines.
* Olive or rapeseed oil.
* Oranges.
* Peanuts.
* Peas.
* Seeds – sunflower, pumpkin.
* Soya or soy beans.
* Sweet potatoes.
* Wholegrain bread.
* Yogurt.

TIP

If you can't eat some of these or you hate them, don't worry! They are just examples and you can find others if you go online or ask a knowledgeable adult. Include as many as you can and enjoy your food!

171

GIVE SLEEP A CHANCE

One of the best things you can do to deal with anxiety is to prioritise your sleep. But the problem is that anxiety makes sleep worse and poor sleep makes anxiety worse. So, if anxiety is keeping you awake, saying you *must* sleep is likely to make you feel more anxious!

There are two ways I can help you. First I'll show you how to make sleep more likely and second I'll show you how to deal with anxiety when it is keeping you awake. Many more details about both these are in my book *The Awesome Power of Sleep* and you will also find useful advice on my website. But here are the essentials.

WHAT TO DO

1. **Where possible, go to bed and get up at roughly the same time every day. Don't go to bed *too* early or have a long lie-in unless you're feeling ill.**

2. **Have a regular winding-down routine: the same actions in the same order at the same time, in the one to two hours before turning your light off.**

3. **During that time, avoid all "sleep negatives" and only do "sleep positives". (See pages 173–4.)**

4. **If you have some big worries, write them down and fold the paper up. Put it out of sight.**

5. **When you get into bed, read a book or listen to music. No screens, other than an ebook reader with notifications off.**

ENJOY SLEEP POSITIVES

Sleep positives are things that make sleep more likely, so you can include them in the one to two hours before you turn your light off. Choose a few and put them into a sensible order. This is now your routine.

WHAT TO DO

* Remove daylight and bright lighting – close curtains and turn off the main light. Just have low lighting, such as a bedside lamp.

* Have a light snack if hungry; nothing too sugary. Perhaps a small sandwich; piece of cheese and fruit; nuts.

* Have a small milky drink or herbal tea.

* Have a shower or bath.

* Change into sleepwear.

* Clean face and brush teeth.

* Listen to soft, slow music.

* Think what went well today; focus on positive thoughts.

* Use lavender oil or sleep balm or spray.

* Do stretches or gentle yoga.

* Do a few minutes of your favourite breathing strategy.

* Organise things ready for the morning.

* Put clothes away or fold them tidily.

* Write journal.

* Write any worries down and then put the paper by the door.

* Draw, doodle or colour in.

* Read for pleasure.

AVOID SLEEP NEGATIVES

Sleep negatives are things that can prevent sleep, so try to avoid all these completely during the one to two hours before turning your light off. An ideal sleeping space is dark, safe, quiet and slightly cool – like a cave.

WHAT TO AVOID

* **Daylight and bright electric light.**
* **Screens (apart from ebook readers – but turn notifications off and dim the light).**
* **Communication with people outside your household – shut the world out; switch your phone off.**
* **The news – it's never relaxing.**
* **Caffeine – coffee, tea and cola drinks (unless caffeine-free).**
* **Energy drinks.**
* **Alcohol – I know you're not drinking it but tell adults it raises heart rate and reduces the deep sleep essential for restoration.**
* **Arguments and stress.**
* **Strenuous exercise that raises the heart rate.**
* **Too much food, and especially any spicy, sugary or rich food.**
* **Loud, fast music.**
* **Noise – try earplugs if necessary.**
* **A messy bedroom.**
* **Being too hot.**
* **Work – it's really important to put it away at least an hour and ideally two hours before bedtime.**

HOW TO STOP ANXIETY FROM KEEPING YOU AWAKE

I am very familiar with worries trying to stop me sleeping. Sometimes worry nearly wins. If I think it's nearly winning, I get up and do something peaceful, like reading in another room, until I'm more tired and then I try again. Worry cannot win for ever!

WHAT TO DO

1. Don't look at the time – it doesn't matter.

2. Don't try too hard to sleep. Sleep comes when your mind and body are ready.

3. Focus on breathing more slowly and relaxing your muscles.

4. Try a meditation strategy – see pages 102–4.

5. Give your mind something other than your worry to focus on. It could be counting backwards, or naming every country you can think of; or thinking about a happy time or planning something fun.

6. If you've been lying there for ages and sleep is nowhere near, get out of bed. Do something quiet (no screens). Go back to bed after a while and relax your body again.

7. Don't worry – no harm will come to you from a bad night.

TIP

It's incredibly common to have phases of poor sleep. But if it often happens and it's making you feel ill or distressed, see a doctor. Do check all the advice on my website, as a doctor will give the same advice first anyway!

USE SCREENS WELL

This is closely connected to my advice on sleep, but screens and devices have some other connections to anxiety so I am also making a separate point.

I love my smartphone, tablet and computer. They are incredibly useful in countless ways. But there are a few big problems with them and you might have experienced any of these already. So, we do sometimes need to switch them off. Because it's difficult, you might need some help. I have some ideas for you on the next page.

First, though, let's be clear about what the problems are. These are the ones I believe are most important and relevant to anxiety:

1. **Our devices are so easy to switch on and there's so much fun to be had on them that it's hard *not* to switch them on. This means that we often use them far too much, including at times when we'd be better not looking at them – for example, when we're trying to work, sleep or think.**

2. **Once we've started scrolling, it's hard to stop, so we find ourselves spending longer than we intended, leaving less time for other important things. Many young people worry about the fact that their screens stop them doing their work.**

3. **Screens can – and very often do – bring us stressful, anxiety-raising messages and images. What we see on social media can be very undermining, lowering self-esteem.**

> **TIP**
> It's most likely that your adults should also use their phones and devices less, so make them read this!

SWITCH YOUR DEVICES OFF

The short version of this strategy is: "Switch them OFF!" But if it was that easy we'd all do it more. How can you make it easier?

Some of these tips apply only to phones; others apply to different devices. Follow whichever apply to the devices you use, so that you can have periods where your peace of mind will not be shattered by a notification.

WHAT TO DO

1. When you don't need your device, put it out of sight and ideally in another room. The harder it is to get it, the more likely you are to stop thinking about it. Research shows that being able to *see* a phone reduces performance on a task.

2. Decide a period of screen-free time and set a timer. Tell yourself why you're doing it and how long for.

3. Make a card that says "OFFLINE TIME" and put it in front of you. When you've finished the offline time, put the card away.

4. Tell people – OK, it's not terribly fascinating for them, but if you announce to key friends, or an online group, or people in your house, that you're going offline for a period of time, it will help.

5. If you have to work at a computer and you need the internet, at least shut down opportunities for notifications, such as email or social media sites.

6. Be positive, not negative. Telling yourself NOT to do something makes you want to do it, so say what you WILL do. "I will do an hour's work offline" is better than "I must not look at my social media for an hour".

MANAGE SOCIAL MEDIA

I mentioned that social media can lower self-esteem. It can also raise anxiety. For some people it's no problem at all but for others it is a big problem.

There are two quite opposite causes of the problem. The first is that you often see versions of perfect lives on social media: the best selfies, biggest successes, the most beautiful holidays, hairstyles, bodies, outfits, experiences. All edited and filtered. You feel that you can never measure up.

The opposite problem is material that is very dark, sad and even terrifying, with images of self-harm or cruel messages, threats and stories that upset and drag you down.

WHAT TO DO

1. **Be self-aware. How is social media making you feel? If it's making you feel bad, you need to stop looking. (Try some of the tips on page 177.)**

2. **Agree with your friends that you'll put phones away from a certain time in the evening. If you know that they're not online either, it's easier to stay offline as you know you aren't missing out.**

3. **If your friends don't want to join you, be proudly different! Put your strongest self out there and just say that social media is bad for your mental health and you want to do something different, something that will move your life forward. You're ambitious, bright, worthy.**

4. **If anything is happening online that is making you feel sad, anxious or distressed, talk to a trusted adult.**

GET SUPPORT

One of the worst things about anxiety is how alone you feel.
You might think that you are the only person feeling as you do,
that no one else could possibly understand, and that you are
tumbling out of control like a twig carried down some rapids.

When you feel like that, it's really important to know
what help is available and how to access it. You are not really
spinning out of control. You're not a twig, for a start: you have
agency. And there are many hands to hold onto, hands that can
really help you and pull you out of the water to dry land. Those
hands *want* to help you, too.

Even if one person seems not to want to help, perhaps
because they have too much on their plate, someone else does.
I promise you that. I can promise it because I know that *I* want
to help you. And I am not alone.

The next few pages show you how to get support when you
need it.

FIND THE RIGHT EARS

Not everyone is good at listening to worries. Although most people want to help, they might not know what to say. And different worries need different ears. If you take your worry to the wrong person, you might not get the help you need. There are things to think about before you ask for support.

WHAT TO DO

1. **Think about the adults you know: parents, carers and other relatives; teachers and support staff; family friends; and other adults such as youth group leaders or sports coaches. Which ones might listen to you? If they don't have the answers, would they know how to guide you to the help you need?**

2. **If you can't find someone appropriate, think about organisations with helplines, such as Childline in the UK (see the Resources section). Or use online chat features on websites that have good advice about the thing you are worried about. Choose recognised organisations that have a good reputation.**

3. **Before contacting anyone, explore and practise the words to express your feelings. See the next page for help with this.**

4. **If speaking to someone face to face, choose a time when the person can listen. If you're not sure, tell them you'd like to talk to them and ask when would be a good time. Tell them it's important and you need them to have the time and headspace to listen.**

5. **You might also share worries with friends, especially worries that you think they might also have. This is a valuable part of friendship. But if you think your friends will not understand or might give poor advice, or it's a very big worry, start with an adult.**

FIND THE RIGHT WORDS

It is not always easy to express ourselves, especially when we're feeling emotional. It's worth spending time thinking how you will express your worry.

WHAT TO DO

1. **Before you talk, think about the following elements of your worry and write down words or phrases:**

   ★ **Time: how long have you been feeling like this?**

   ★ **Frequency: how often is it a problem for you? Once a day, every now and then, in phases, many times a day, only at night?**

   ★ **What parts of your life is it affecting? Concentration, friendships, family relationships, grades, sleep, self-esteem, eating, mood, ambition, decision-making, feelings about the future, physical health?**

   ★ **What words would you use to describe how you feel: scared, terrified, jittery, anxious, gloomy, sad, angry, confused, overwhelmed, alone?**

   ★ **Do certain things trigger these feelings or do they happen at any time? When you've been out with friends? When you've been online? When you hear people arguing?**

2. **Thinking about those answers, can you sum up your worry in two or three sentences? Write them down.**

3. **Think about what you would like the result of your conversation to be. For example, do you want to find out where you can access other help? Do you want reassurance or strategies? Do you want to feel less alone?**

4. **Take your notes with you when you talk to your chosen person.**

PROFESSIONAL HELP

This book will certainly help you but if anxiety feels too much for you or is spoiling your life and damaging your ability to succeed, professional advice could also be needed. Reading this book first will help you in three ways. You will understand what anxiety is and that it is natural and normal to feel anxious – sometimes very anxious. You will find ideas to try on your own while waiting for personal advice. You will develop the language to describe your anxieties when you meet a mental health professional. If you feel you need to seek further help, here is some advice.

WHAT TO DO

1. **If you can, talk to your family doctor. In the UK you can make an appointment yourself if you wish. The doctor will not share what you've said with your parents or carers unless you agree. (If the doctor thinks you are in danger, they must act on this but they will discuss with you.) If you find it hard to get an appointment, don't give up – sometimes we have to keep asking.**

2. **You can contact Childline (in the UK) or similar organisations in your country for advice and support.**

3. **Ask if your school has a counsellor.**

4. **If your anxiety is about a specific thing – such as LGBTQ+ issues, self-harm, alcohol, drugs, sex or bullying – seek out a relevant and recognised organisation in your country.**

IMPORTANT

If you think about taking your own life or have investigated this, tell an adult immediately. In the UK, you can contact the Samaritans: phone 116 123 day or night.

WHAT ABOUT MEDICATION?

There are drugs which can help reduce anxiety but doctors are rightly very cautious about prescribing them, particularly to young people. Developing brains – as yours is – do not respond in quite the same way to some substances as adult brains and there is still too much we don't know. Also, some medications lead to dependency and addiction.

Antidepressants are sometimes prescribed for anxiety, as anxiety and depression are often closely linked. But these are among that group of drugs that can have different effects in young brains. Your doctor is likely to want to try various other treatments before using medication.

For these reasons, it is incredibly important that you only ever take a prescription-only drug when it has been prescribed for *you* (not for someone else who you think has the same symptoms) by a suitably qualified medical practitioner. You should also take any medication exactly as prescribed and let your doctor know about any side effects or if you feel worse in any way, mentally or physically.

What about "over-the-counter" herbal remedies? The fact that it is possible to buy them without prescription doesn't mean they can't be harmful. You should only try these after consulting your doctor as they can have unwanted effects, cause dependency or react negatively with other drugs you are taking or conditions you have.

YOUR CHOSEN STRATEGIES

Now it's time to pull together what you've learnt! You know that different strategies work for different people. And you've had a chance to try out various ones for yourself. You've probably decided which breathing and grounding strategies you like best and you've probably had many moments when you've thought, "I like the idea of that – I think that would work for me." But how will you remember which ones to use when you're *actually* feeling anxious?

WHAT TO DO

1. Go through all the strategies, using the list on on pages 74–5 to direct you to the ones you want, and on paper or screen jot down the ones that work well for you or that you'd like to try.

2. Then get a big piece of paper – it's better to do this than use a computer – and make a colourful, bold poster of your chosen activities. Group them with headings such as "instant actions" or "distraction activities".

3. Decorate it however you want. Pin it to your bedroom wall.

4. You're ready to tame anxiety any time it barks at you!

FINALLY...

You have learnt so much and come so far! This is the beginning of a new life for you: you can use the skills you've learnt and be proud each time you do. You'll get better at managing worries, partly as you get older, partly as you experience that you *do* cope and partly as you practise everything you've learnt from this book.

Here are the key messages you now understand:

1. Everyone worries and is anxious sometimes but it's more of a challenge for some of you, perhaps because you have more worries right now or perhaps because your brain just reacts more strongly to worry.

2. Anxiety itself is not a problem or illness but how your body and mind react to anxiety can *become* a problem. It can make you feel rubbish and can have a negative effect on your life. That's a problem you'll want to solve – and now you can.

3. Anxiety and panic cannot really harm you. Your body is overreacting to a fear your brain believes is there.

4. Avoiding the things you fear does not make you fear them less. The trick is to learn to manage your reactions so that you can take on the challenges and face down the fears. You can say "No worries!" to your worries.

5. Once you understand what anxiety is and how it affects you, you can choose the strategies that will be your defence. Sometimes you will choose relaxation actions such as breathing techniques, grounding exercises or meditation tools; sometimes you will choose distraction actions, to take your mind away from anxiety and into useful, positive interests or hobbies. This book has shown you how to make those choices and given you lots of ideas.

In short, you have learnt that anxiety is like a guard dog – your personal guard dog. At first it wasn't well trained: it growled at everything, even tiny things, and sometimes it growled at you. Sometimes you ran away from it or overreacted to it and it responded by chasing you and barking even more.

Now you know how to tame your guard dog, so it only barks to warn you of possible danger, to defend you and keep you safe. And when it growls and you feel anxious, you will look more closely at what it's growling at; you will be able to assess whether you *are* in danger – usually not – and what to do about it. You'll be able to tell your guard dog that you're ready to deal with the situation and now, please, stop barking. Reacting to the thought of danger or the possibility of it is what your guard dog is supposed to do, but then you take charge and say to it, "Calm down now. I can handle this."

You are – or you can be – the ruler of your mind. You won't always feel that you are and sometimes life will throw challenges at you that will make it extra hard. But you can become stronger and more confident, learning the tricks you need. You can tackle anxiety, not by screaming at it in fear or running away but by respecting it, harnessing it and living alongside it while it does its job of keeping you safe. Good guard dog!

If I can do this, so can you. I can. You can. We can. No worries.

PERSONAL EXPERIENCES OF ANXIETY

Almost everything you've read in this book has been either about how people in general experience anxiety or how you personally are experiencing anxiety. But I believe it's really useful to hear actual stories from other people, real people who have experienced things that might be the same or different from what you or I feel. When we hear other people's experiences, it builds our own empathy, helps us understand ourselves and also opens our mind. Real stories are so meaningful and they build powerful connections in your brain.

So, when I was writing this book, I asked if any adults who had personal experience of anxiety, in themselves or their children, would be willing to share their experiences and ideas. Here's what they said and I'm very grateful to them. I've changed all the names. Except the first one – that's me!

NICOLA – "BEING HEARD IS INCREDIBLY IMPORTANT"

I would call myself an anxious person. As a child, I was put on an anti-anxiety medication which would not be used now and in my thirties I benefited from a counsellor. Being heard is incredibly important. But I just feel I'm naturally anxious, not ill. For me, it's part of being sensitive, thinking, ambitious, wanting to do better. I wouldn't want to change how I am, only practise reacting more usefully.

I've learnt most from reading sensible words, talking to experts, and applying what I've learnt to observing myself. I've learnt why humans act, think and feel as we do. I've learnt to spot patterns in my thinking and when I'm in a worry phase I remind myself that right now my thinking is dodgy and doesn't reflect external reality. My anxious phases usually begin with things I wish I hadn't said or done, or things I haven't done as well as I wanted, but then spiral into worrying about anything.

Things that help me most: reminding myself of good things about myself and my life; enjoying nature; doing something positive like going for a run, reading, cooking or taking time to give myself a hand or foot massage. I think mood involves a balancing act – when we see our mood tipping too far towards the negative (anxiety or sadness or anger or whatever), we need to take *positive* actions to push the scales back towards a balanced middle. The key is in first recognising that we're tipping in the wrong direction, then knowing what actions will tip us back – and then doing them!

I always thought I was very bad at relaxing, despite the fact that I teach people how to relax so I obviously know *how* to. But recently I had a test to measure how calm my heart rate is when I'm trying to relax. I was astonished to get a perfect score! Interestingly, while I was doing the test I was imagining being in a particular bit of my garden looking at the flowers, trees and hills. I need to remember that the simplest things – even just thinking about something I love – can be my way to a healthier mind.

SHAHEEN - "I WISH I WAS MORE LIKE MY DAUGHTER"

When I was growing up, I worried all the time – about art lessons, PE lessons, my looks, my parents' arguments, exam results, my mother's mental health, friendships, my future, everything. My worries continue but I think I manage them better, by gardening and having talking therapy, for example. I had CBT (Cognitive Behavioural Therapy) for social anxiety some years ago and it really helped.

I thought about anxiety recently because of my thirteen-year-old daughter. She is normally very relaxed but then she was injured and as a result missed a lot of school. During her phased return, she didn't want to go to a particular lesson because she would feel left behind. We talked through it and my husband suggested she buddy with someone, so she attended the lesson and it was OK – not great, but manageable. I thought how good it is that young people now have a name for their worries and can talk about it.

As to why my daughter is so relaxed, I think it is a combination of nature and nurture. My husband is laid-back and confident, so I suspect genetics plays a part. I made practical changes to be present for my daughter. I had saved up financially to be at home until she was six and I then took a local term-time job which enabled me to be around for her. (She doesn't have any siblings.) I shielded her from conflict, whereas my mother overshared. My daughter has resilience, I think, because she knows she is well supported, by me and my husband, her aunt and grandparents. (She is the only grandchild on both sides of the family.) I wish I was more like her.

NOTE FROM NICOLA: Genetics might play a part but also children do imitate the adults and others around them. I definitely agree that Shaheen's daughter is helped by feeling secure in the support of the adults in her family. However young or old we are we need to feel there are people who have our back.

MARY – "I LOST MY TEENS TO PANIC DISORDER"

I had my first panic attack aged ten in hospital after having my appendix out. I lost my teens to panic disorder which, untreated, developed into depression, but was rescued aged eighteen by a new doctor and an antidepressant. Panic disorder wasn't recognised as a medical condition until 1980 and in 1954 my doctor hadn't a clue. I had a severe episode a couple of years ago after a mega-stressful house move. My current antidepressant is working wonders.

> **NOTE FROM NICOLA:** Antidepressants *can* work well for anxiety (see page 183). They do have different effects on children and adolescents, though, so should only be prescribed with great care. Never take medications unless prescribed for you by a doctor.

EMMA - "I BECAME ANXIOUS ABOUT THINGS I USED TO DO EASILY"

A series of big life events (two bereavements plus a sudden and serious illness in a family member) led to me suffering generalised anxiety. It was suggested that it might be mild Post-Traumatic Stress Disorder (PTSD) but I never had an official diagnosis.

My anxiety went beyond fear of illness and death (although that was absolutely a part of it) and I began to find other things quite challenging. For example, going on a long drive, something I had done regularly, suddenly became something I had to psych myself up for. The best way I can describe my mental state is that I was "constantly waiting for the other shoe to drop". It's like the rug was pulled out from under me and all sense of safety evaporated. Horrible!

Things that have helped considerably: being outside, either walking in local woodland or working in my garden; gratitude, listing all the things that are going well in my life; breathwork; listening to guided meditations or nature sounds whilst lying on an acupressure mat; remembering to be kind to myself.

My breathwork was usually a variation on triangle breathing (see page 81). It sometimes helped to place a hand over my heart and mentally repeat a mantra of some kind, something as simple as "I am safe". I think the key point here was becoming aware of the fact that a stressed state leads to shallow breathing and making sure I learnt to pay attention to my physical needs and deliberately relax my body.

NOTE FROM NICOLA: Distressing life events can lead someone who wasn't particularly anxious before to suffer anxiety that doesn't seem directly linked to the events. Emma describes a clear example of someone getting into worry chains (see page 49) triggered by something different. And she demonstrates a great use of positive strategies.

ALEX - "IN SCHOOL WE WORK ON BREATHING TECHNIQUES"

I have suffered from anxiety and have found that a good sleep routine, exercise, deep breathing and meditation are all extremely helpful. As a teacher, I have also worked with young people who are anxious and I find they often overestimate the problem and underestimate the resources they have to deal with it. So we look at their strengths and skills, brainstorm possible solutions and challenge unhelpful thinking styles. We also experiment with different coping strategies so that they can find out what works for them. Doing something creative can be very soothing.

In school we work on breathing techniques – I show them lots of different things but I particularly like hot chocolate breathing because it emphasises the need for a long exhale. I also like 4-7-8 breathing, square breathing and five-finger breathing.

I do think we teach a lot more to support young people's mental health than we used to even five years ago, and certainly much more than twenty years ago! Still, a lot of children continue to suffer from anxiety, and the mental health services can't cope with demand, so it falls to us to try and do something.

NOTE FROM NICOLA: Great to see a teacher using their own experience of anxiety to help students. You'll find those breathing strategies described on pages 79–85.

SAM - "I'M A BIG BELIEVER IN LETTING HER SET HER OWN GOALS"

My daughter, Jen, had a big problem with anxiety a few years ago. There was no particular trigger, though the school link worker suggested it was a delayed reaction to my husband and me splitting up. She became obsessed with water, constantly drinking to the point at which she would vomit. I withdrew her from school and allowed her twenty millilitres every ten minutes, which to start with she found INCREDIBLY difficult. It was exhausting but eventually she got through it and her anxiety became really very low for a couple of years.

Then we all got Covid and I was too ill to look after her so she couldn't be with me. Her anxiety built up again and she started to struggle at school. So I pulled her out again. Last term she started back doing partial days, gradually building up. Now she's doing brilliantly at school but her anxiety levels at home seem to be rising. It's like the anxiety is one of those squishy balls – you squeeze it in your hand and lumps bulge out at either end.

"School refusal" and "school phobia" don't fit Jen's problem because it's not school that's the issue. It's as though her comfort zone expands and shrinks. If it's very small, ANYTHING can be a problem. When she was off school I had to go to the dentist, and they said she couldn't come in with me because of Covid. She sat in the waiting room and, although she made it, she was supremely uncomfortable. On another day she wouldn't have minded at all. So I would say she has "generalised anxiety", and it just so happens that since she's supposed to go to school five days a week, that's going to be the biggest area of challenge.

She's on the waiting list for CAMHS (Child and Adolescent Mental Health Services). She has particular triggers that don't seem to get easier – spitting out after brushing teeth is one. She can't look and I have to hold her hand while she does it. She has terrible emetophobia, which was another problem in school in the winter months.

We've found being able to laugh at something helps enormously. We went to Disneyland and there were several issues with various rides but the Star Tours one proved an unexpected success, because it was humorous.

I'm a big believer in letting her set her own goals. When given enough flexibility to choose, she'll often challenge herself. She's been very anxious about the end of term performance and sometimes had to sit out of rehearsals. I told her form tutor that I wanted her to have the option NOT to perform and he let her operate the CD player in rehearsals. Today was the first performance and her dad has just sent through a video of her actually singing with all the others. I know it's because she knew she didn't have to.

I do feel that sometimes kids are made more anxious by well-meaning people insisting "just try it". If you say to a kid "you don't have to" and let them feel it REALLY doesn't matter, then I'm sure it reduces the anxiety.

NOTE FROM NICOLA: Sam has great insight about Jen's anxiety but I really hope they get the CAMHS appointment soon, to show Jen how to face the everyday things that distress her. Laughter and setting her own goals are great strategies in the meantime. The more Jen experiences that she *can* do things, the more able she will be to cope.

CONNOR - "I WAS CURED BY THE GP TELLING ME IT WAS VERY COMMON"

I suffered from anxiety for a couple of years in my early to mid-thirties. What is interesting is I had no good reason. I was single, living abroad, great job, friends, lifestyle, with lots of sport and socialising. I'd had lots of relationships but was still single and frankly, despite having great friends, I was lonely.

This was mostly after big party nights out. The next day I felt alone and then I'd question where I was going with my life. I even got anxious about my job security, my skill set, my confidence, my ability to find the right person to have a loving relationship with. At that time, mental illness was taboo so I was afraid to speak to anyone, compounding the situation. It affected me badly, with panic attacks, lack of confidence, loss of appetite, sweating in social situations, generally feeling lost.

I turned a corner when I returned home to visit my family and had to turn down a social event as I was feeling so bad. I opened up with my sister and then went to the family GP. The GP was super clear: I was suffering from anxiety and panic attacks. I was cured by him telling me it was very common and he could offer medication to halt the downward spiral. This addressed my biggest fear which was about losing control and never being cured. In fact, I ended up not needing the medication but the knowledge that it was there helped me in the months and years ahead to fully recover and rebuild my confidence.

NOTE FROM NICOLA: Connor says he had "no good reason" to feel anxious – but feeling lonely and worrying about the future are good reasons! It's quite common for people to think, "But I'm so lucky – I shouldn't feel so bad – I must be stupid or going mad!" No, just human, lost and alone. I'm glad he talked to his sister and that his GP was brilliant. Note that Connor didn't take his medication, which turned out to be a good decision for him but this was in consultation with a sympathetic GP. Talk to your GP if you are in doubt about something you've been prescribed. Never stop medication without discussing with your doctor first.

DIANE – "I WAS ABLE TO IDENTIFY MY TRIGGERS"

I was diagnosed with severe anxiety attacks at the age of ten. I would hyperventilate and shake and my hands would spasm. In my twenties a sympathetic doctor explained what was happening and helped me control it with breathing exercises and techniques. I had fewer attacks through my thirties, although they began to show themselves in two different ways: although I could get my breathing under control, I couldn't do anything when they manifested as extreme upset stomachs and on occasions I would be sick. These occasions have always been more distressing than the other kind.

In my thirties and forties I was able to identify my triggers and prepare better for the possibility of anxiety attacks. My doctor told me that it is better to experience a panic attack outwardly and know how to control it than allow it to manifest itself internally. This idea freed me to see anxiety as normal but just that mine happens to look like this.

My anxiety attacks happen *after* a stress has occurred, sometimes days later. They start in my stomach and I know within a split second that I am about to have one. I experience a nauseous sensation creeping up me. It feels like my stomach has flipped over and the acidity in my stomach has become alkaline. When it reaches my neck and face I go red and tingly, my vision sometimes narrows and I get sweaty. As soon as I feel the first symptom I remove myself if I can and do my breathing techniques, and I tap (see note on EFT below). I can usually bring it back quite quickly to normal but I will feel the chemical changes in my body for 24 to 36 hours.

I was introduced to tapping many years ago and I find it does help me. I was also a massage therapist and trainer so learnt how to do acupressure facial massage. I use this technique often if I get headaches or feel stressed.

My doctor helped me to understand that anxiety is a natural response and that I shouldn't be afraid of it. Once I identified my triggers, I could learn how to prepare for potentially stressful situations and if one happened when I was with people, how to manage it. I have never felt like a victim of these attacks and never let them limit me.

NOTE FROM NICOLA: Diane's experience is interesting because her anxiety shows itself quite a time after the actual trigger and her symptoms are strongly physical. With excellent professional help, she's come to understand her individual responses and to become better prepared and able to reduce them. EFT or Tapping (see pages 105–6) has also helped her so she has managed this quite severe anxiety without using medication. Her anxiety symptoms do not stop her leading a full and exciting life.

You can see that all these adults have had a range of different experiences and you can also see how much they've learnt about themselves and how to manage their anxiety. None of them had much advice or help when they were at school but nowadays there's a lot of wisdom and support for you. We know so much more about anxiety and how to treat it than we did when I and the other adults were young. So, although young people in general tend to have more causes of stress – because of social media and the other pressures of modern life – you do also have more people able and willing to listen to you and share what they've learnt. Let us help! We are here for you.

RESOURCES

Free helplines for immediate or urgent advice:
Childline (UK) – 0800 1111 – or you can chat online:
www.childline.org.uk
Samaritans (UK) – 116 123 – or online: www.samaritans.org
Your country should have its own helpline.

Contacting your GP (in the UK)
The best thing is to tell your parent or carer that you'd like to talk to a GP about your anxiety symptoms. But you are allowed to make an appointment yourself, if you prefer. A GP will not discuss what you say with your parents or carers unless you agree to this. They might need to talk to an appropriate person if they feel that you or someone else is in danger. They would also discuss this with you.

If for any reason a GP appointment is not what you want, try one of the helplines above or websites below.

Useful websites
The Anna Freud National Centre for Children and Families has a huge amount of really useful information on a vast range of topics:
www.annafreud.org/on-my-mind/self-care/

Beyond Blue is an Australian site focusing on many aspects of mental health: www.beyondblue.org.au
There is a helpline for residents of Australia but the information is great wherever you are.

I'm Enough is an international site dedicated to helping people avoid or deal with distress specifically from social media and digital technology:
www.imenough.co

Mind is a UK-based mental health charity: www.mind.org.uk

Teens Health is a US website with lots of great advice for teenagers: www.teenshealth.org

Young Minds is a UK mental health charity aimed at young people and the adults who care about them: www.youngminds.org.uk

The Scottish NHS has a useful set of information here: www.nhsinform.scot/illnesses-and-conditions/mental-health/anxiety

Books about anxiety and stress
The Teenage Guide to Stress (by me) – see also my books, *Body Brilliant* (includes advice about body dysmorphia and eating disorders), *Exam Attack* (for anxiety about exams) and *Be Resilient*.

Be Happy Be You by Penny Alexander and Becky Goddard-Hill
The Worry (Less) Book by Rachel Brian
Learn to Stress Less by Dr Vee Freir
Fighting Invisible Tigers by Earl Hipp
The 7 Habits of Highly Effective Teens by Sean Covey
The Anxiety Workbook for Teens by Lisa M Schab

Resources mentioned in *No Worries*
I have listed these in the order in which they appear in the book.

Neuroticism
Neuroticism is one of the "Big Five" personality traits – if you'd like to find out more you could start with these:

Psychology Today: www.psychologytoday.com/gb/basics/neuroticism

PsyCom: www.psycom.net/neuroticism

Type A and Type B personalities
For more on these, start here with Simply Psychology: www.simplypsychology.org/personality-a.html

(Be cautious if using free online personality tests. Many require your email address and some are not suitable for young people because they include questions about driving, household bills, careers, adult relationships. Discuss with an adult. They might like to do them, too!)

The START method
Information about Dr Vee Freir and links to her books are available on her website (www.dr-vee.co.uk) and on Amazon.

Belly breathing
A YouTube video from Nemours.org:
www.youtube.com/watch?v=_xQJ2O4b5TM/

Mindfulness and meditation
It's easy to find information about mindfulness and meditation but hard to find things actually aimed at you rather than your teachers and parents or carers. Here are some resources I like:

Mindfulness for Teens: www.mindfulnessforteens.com

Mental Up: www.mentalup.co/blog/mindfulness-activities-for-teens

Girl Guiding has some nice activities equally for girls and boys:
www.girlguiding.org.uk/what-we-do/our-stories-and-news/blogs/5-creative-ways-to-find-calm/

The Mindfulness Teacher YouTube channel has lots of videos, some of which are for very young children but many are appropriate for anyone:
www.youtube.com/c/TheMentalHealthTeacher

Headspace is a well-known app for mindfulness, meditation and breathing, with sections on stress and sleep, too. Unfortunately, it's not free (though there's a free trial which would teach you the basics):
www.headspace.com

Insight Timer and Mindfulness Coach are two examples of well-known apps that are free at the moment. But I suggest you look for well-reviewed apps by searching "free guided meditation" and make sure it's not just a free trial you're signing up to. (I believe, of course, that people should be able to charge for things they've created, but I prefer it when there's a free, simple version and a paid, ad-free version that is completely optional.)

EFT – tapping

Tap Within has a good free handout with instructions: www.tapwithin.com

The Tapping Solution has a lot of information and resources including an app (currently free but has in-app purchases and the usual annoying adverts): www.thetappingsolution.com/tapping-101/

Healthline has this clear explanation and instructions: www.healthline.com/health/eft-tapping

Readaxation and reading for pleasure

Readaxation is a concept I came up with. Some schools use readaxation as a regular thing, with special lunchtimes, for example – ask your school librarian! Here are some resources on my website for you to investigate further:

On www.nicolamorgan.com search "reading brain" and also "readaxation".

On www.nicolamorgan.com/core-resource-the-reading-brain/, you'll find a link to a report by The Reading Agency in 2015, which looked at hundreds of other studies and pieces of research from around the world and listed the benefits we can safely say come from regularly reading for pleasure.

If you want to measure how well reading helps you relax, search for my "Readaxation Diary" tool!

I've put together a list of wonderful, positive, uplifting and anxiety-lowering novels you might read to reassure you. On my website, search "Reading to reduce anxiety".

Cognitive Behavioural Therapy – CBT

There is an enormous amount about CBT online, most of it written for adults. Here are good resources for you:

Young Minds has a section on talking therapies and CBT has a small section there: www.youngminds.org.uk/young-person/your-guide-to-support/counselling-and-therapy

Happier Human has some anxiety worksheets for young people, based on CBT approaches: www.happierhuman.com/anxiety-worksheets/

And I recommend *The Anxiety Workbook for Teens* mentioned above.

My pathways exercise

There's an explanatory post on my website – www.nicolamorgan.com/wellbeing-and-stress-management/positive-pathways-brain-practical-wellbeing/ – which includes a link to a Powerpoint.

Character strengths and "What went well"

Martin Seligman's character strengths are at www.viacharacter.org, where you will also find a quiz to assess your personal strengths, as well as links to his research into the "What went well" activity.

Spirituality and faith

I mentioned that research suggests that having a spiritual aspect to your life might have a benefit for mental health. See Religion, Spirituality and Health: the research and clinical implications: https://www.ncbi.nlm.nih.gov/pmc/articles/PMC3671693/

Social anxiety

The UK's NHS has a good and reassuring explanation:
www.nhs.uk/mental-health/conditions/social-anxiety/

CBT Psychology has these Seven Tips for Teens With Social Anxiety:
https://cbtpsychology.com/7-tips-teens-with-social-anxiety/

Introversion

Susan Cain is the best-known writer on this topic. Her website, Quiet Revolution – www.quietrev.com – will give you lots of information and support and a good test to measure your introversion. (See the drop-down menu for "Quiet" and scroll down.) Her second book, *Quiet Power*, is a brilliant resource with practical strategies for introverts in school settings.

Scarcity

I mentioned a book – it's written for adults: *Scarcity – Why having too little means so much* by Sendhil Mullainathan and Eldar Shafir. In this excerpt they explain how they came to the idea:
www.behavioralscientist.org/scarcity-excerpt-mullainathan-shafir/

Getting Things Done – GTD

Here's an explanation on the website of the author, David Allen, who created the GTD concept: www.gettingthingsdone.com/what-is-gtd/

The app that I use is Todoist – www.todoist.com. You can use it free in a limited way but that could well be enough for most people. It was through Todoist that the concept of GTD came to my attention and through that I found David Allen's work.

Yoga

Yoga Ed has a nice introductory video for teenagers here:
www.youtube.com/watch?v=_f8nfwlcK-g/

T'ai chi

Leia Cohen at Taiflow has a great beginner video here introducing a "five minutes a day" practice:
www.youtube.com/watch?v=cEOS2z0yQw4/
You can subscribe free to her newsletter and get weekly videos:
www.youtube.com/c/Taiflow

Sleep

I've written a book on sleep, *The Awesome Power of Sleep*, which is for teenagers and adults. On my website (www.nicolamorgan.com) you will find various free resources and lots of posts. On the Books page, choose the book and scroll down for lots of downloadable and shareable items.

Screens

My book *The Teenage Guide to Life Online* will tell you all you need to know about the positives and negatives of screens, including problems with anxiety, and give you lots of help on how to avoid the negatives.

Again, on my website there's lots of free advice and resources, including the Life Online Parent Pack. Go to www.nicolamorgan.com and visit the page for the book (under the Books heading).

GENERAL INDEX

INDEX OF STRATEGIES

ACKNOWLEDGEMENTS

I gratefully acknowledge the contribution of all who shared their experiences of anxiety with me; the expertise and empathy of psychologist Dr Vee Freir; the anxiety-reducing voice of Elizabeth Roy, my literary agent since 2001; and all the people of various ages I've listened to and learnt from over the years. By building my understanding of humans, you are all part of this book.

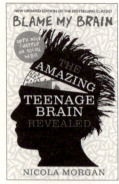